Waterfalls
of Minnesota

by Lisa Crayford

Adventure Publications
Cambridge, Minnesota

Acknowledgments

I would like to thank my #1 hiking buddy, Sue Dropp, for all your inspiration and laughs along the trails. Thank you, Rachel Brehmer for making all our hikes fun and bug-free with your homemade bug spray. To my daughters, Nora and Sophie, thank you for never giving up. You just keep going and going like little Energizer bunnies. You have seen more of Minnesota than most Minnesotans! A huge thank you to my hiking and canoeing buddy, Jessica Rogholt, for pushing my hiking limits and for helping me get some amazing waterfall images on the north shore and up in the BWCA.

Thank you to these great ladies for helping me (a photographer and not a writer) with my wordage and correct punctuation: Mechele Pitchford gave me great advice from the start; Julie Dengerud and Kathy Siegler read some of my stories and proofed them for me. It was always good to hear Kathy say, "It makes me want to go there."

Finally, a big thank you to all these helpful friends and good people in my life: Stephenie, Madison and Grace Hiivala; Gary Alan Nelson; Eve Wallinga; Stan Tekiela; Jim and Judy Brandenburg; Quinn from Bearskin Lodge; Adam from Gunflint Lodge; Jason and Josh at Hungry Jack Lodge; Brian Leither; Heidi Veith; Jules' Bistro; April Mastey; Cindy Johnson; Tracy Clark; Teresa Kohls; the staff at Adventure Publishing; Douglas Feltman; Travis Novitsky; Bryan Hansel; Chris Crayford and Carol Kadelbach.

Dedication

To Sue, Nora and Sophie
All photos by Lisa Crayford
Cover photo: Bridal Falls

Edited by Brett Ortler
Cover and book design by Lora Westberg

10 9 8 7 6 5 4 3 2 1

Copyright 2016 by Lisa Crayford
Published by Adventure Publications
820 Cleveland Street South
Cambridge, Minnesota 55008
(800) 678-7006
www.adventurepublications.net
ISBN: 978-1-59193-579-7; eISBN: 978-1-59193-612-1

Preface

It's hard to really pinpoint my beginning love of waterfalls. In 1998, when I was 24, my husband, Chris, and I traveled to the big island of Hawaii and to Maui. At every hairpin turn on the road to Hana, we pulled our Mustang convertible over to the side. I just had to photograph all of the unbelievable waterfalls.

Now fast-forward to April 2012. I have my own professional portrait photography studio in central Minnesota and I have two young daughters. If you're a portrait photographer in Minnesota, April tends to be a pretty boring month, and it's not too pretty outside. So I decided to give myself an assignment to "photograph Minnesota." I know this is not a small task. I tend to do things on a large scale with most of my ideas anyway.

My girls, Nora and Sophie, and I started exploring our fabulous state, reaching every corner in 2012. Since then, we have stayed at many awesome resorts and cabins, and we've met some great people. My girls have hopped up on many roadside statues, and we've seen most of the 26 Paul Bunyans found in our state.

In January 2015 I figured it was time to put all these Minnesota images to work. I wanted to put together a high-quality photography book. Traveling with my girls has led me to many gift shops, where I found many, many books about Minnesota. Most of the books that I really liked were published by the same company, Adventure Publishing out of Cambridge, Minnesota. So I contacted them in January, not knowing what road to take with my book ideas. They helped me produce this book: *Waterfalls of Minnesota*.

I hope you will use this as your guide to many fun and adventurous hikes throughout our wonderful state. Enjoy every step of your waterfall journeys and try to take time to journal and photograph along the way. And don't forget to read my 11 tips on photographing waterfalls. They will help you capture beautiful waterfall images that will justify a long hike deep into the woods.

Safe & Happy Travels,

Lisa

Table of Contents

What Is a Waterfall and How Does It Work?

You probably remember the basics of how rivers work from your seventh-grade science class: Rivers and streams flow downhill because of gravity, and they flow downstream until they merge with another body of water, whether it's another river, a lake or the ocean. Waterfalls form when those rivers flow over a layer of hard rock, like granite, that is situated atop a thick layer of a softer rock. Over the course of the stream or river, the water descends over a ledge, and over time, this water flowing over the ledge begins to erode the softer rock beneath, undercutting the bottom layer. This makes the drop even taller, and eventually large chunks of the resulting overhang collapse into the deepening pool below, accelerating the process. Now the next part may seem a bit strange: Waterfalls are essentially temporary. They are always in retreat, gouging out the softer rock beneath them. Eventually, they collapse, forming a steep section of the river.

Minnesota's Waterfalls

While there are waterfalls located all over the state, many of Minnesota's waterfalls are situated in the north and northeast. This is no surprise, given that the area is home to some of Minnesota's most dramatic topography, not to mention all of the myriad rivers and streams that flow into Lake Superior and the region's thousands of lakes. Still, there are plenty of waterfalls around the rest of the state, including some in the heart of the metro area.

A Note About Seasonal Variations

One of the best parts about waterfalls is that they're always different. Water levels are always fluctuating, and this is especially true seasonally. The gentle tumble of water you see surrounded by falling leaves in autumn can easily become an unrecognizable torrent amid the spring runoff. In winter, the falls get even weirder yet, sometimes freezing entirely, sometimes partially, and always presenting an otherworldly sight that is great to view from a distance (and away from the always sketchy river ice). So if the falls you visit in this book don't look like the picture that I took, visit again in a different season, and then again, and get to know the many different moods each waterfall has to offer.

Trespassing and Waterfall Viewing

All of the waterfalls in this book are either on public land or accessible if you pay admission. A few of the waterfalls included are located on private land but are accessible to the public via another means (by boat, for instance). When you go waterfalling, always be aware of your surroundings and don't venture onto private land unless you've received prior permission.

The Boundary Waters Canoe Area Wilderness and State or Local Parks

Many of the waterfalls in this book are located in the BWCAW, or in one of Minnesota's many fine state or local parks. Because the BWCAW is designated as a national wilderness area, the number of visitors to the area is strictly controlled via a permitting process. There are several varieties of permits—day-use passes are free, but still required—but if you're staying overnight, you'll need to reserve your permit, often well in advance. You'll also have to pay a fee. For all the details on the permitting process, visit www.recreation.gov.

Similarly, if you're parking at a state park, you'll need to purchase a $5 day pass or a $25 annual pass, which gives you access to every other state park. (Note: There are a few waysides where you can park on Hwy. 61 for free and then hike into the park, but if you're parking on state park grounds, you'll need to pay for the day pass.)

Waterfall Safety

Waterfalls are awe-inspiring sights, but they can also be dangerous. A number of deaths have occurred due to waterfall-related accidents. When you visit a waterfall, it's best to stay on the beaten path, if at all possible. If that doesn't exist, you need to use caution, especially if you opt to scramble down to get a closer look or head down to river level. If you do so, realize that you're taking a risk. Always be aware of the water levels, and don't approach a river if the water level is up, as you're liable to be swept away. Always steer clear of dams, too, as these seemingly harmless-looking structures can be death traps if water levels are up.

On a similar note, if the water levels are lower and you opt to swim, use caution and don't go alone, and always avoid cliff jumping or other needlessly risky activity.

What to Bring

Most people consider these 10 items essential: matches, a compass, a map, a knife, a flashlight, sunglasses, fire kindling, extra food, extra clothing, and a first-aid kit. Add plastic baggies to the list for waterproofing and organizing.

And be sure to carry an adequate supply of water. Don't drink any surface water unless it has been boiled for 1 minute or treated. Do not count on a cell phone for your safety. Wireless reception may be spotty or nonexistent on the trail, even on a waterfall walk near a town or interstate.

The preceding list may seem long, but the first six essentials can fit into a plastic bag. Extra food and clothing (a few candy bars and a raincoat or fleece) don't take up much space. Avid hikers sometimes keep a day pack filled and ready to go. Check the contents occasionally, testing batteries, restocking first-aid supplies, and adding to food reserves as necessary.

Photographing Waterfalls

I photograph every waterfall I visit, preserving the images on my computer and printing and framing my favorites. Not all the photographs I take of waterfalls are great; some are just snapshots to preserve a memory. I've spent a lot of time photographing waterfalls, but getting an excellent waterfall image takes time and effort.

To get great images, you need a tripod, a digital camera with manual settings, and early-morning or late-afternoon light. Capturing the personality of a waterfall may mean several visits during different times of the year. The photographs in this book are the result of years of hard work, early-morning wake-up calls, and lots of hiking. In the process, I gained some solid insight that relates directly to waterfall photography. Here is a summary of the basics:

Tripod: You'll need a sturdy tripod because you can't hold a camera sufficiently steady when using slow shutter speeds. Be sure the tripod is compact and lightweight, as you'll be carrying it along with you on your hike. If you want to know when to use a tripod, here's our rough rule of thumb: Use a tripod whenever you can, especially if the shutter speed is less than the lens focal length. For example, don't handhold a 50-millimeter lens when using a shutter speed slower than 1/60 of a second.

Cable Release/Timer: When you're taking a photo, use a cable release, which is a cord attached to the shutter button that separates you from the camera, or use your built-in camera timer. Both of these options reduce the vibration that's caused by pressing the shutter button.

ISO Speed: The ISO setting on most modern digital cameras is designed to approximate the ISO speed of film used in a traditional camera. The lowest ISO number you'll find on a digital camera—usually 100 but sometimes lower—is generally the best setting for shooting waterfalls, as it will yield the greatest detail, sharpness, effects, and color accuracy.

Shutter Speed: Slow shutter speeds give a sense of movement. Mike Wyatt, in his book *Basic Essentials of Photography Outdoors,* explains how shutter speed relates to moving current: "The movement of flowing water will be completely stopped at 1/2000 second. The fastest portions of the water will begin to soften at 1/60 second. At 1/15 second, the water's movement will be clearly evident, but the water will not be completely blurred." Most waterfall photographs are shot at 1/8 second or slower to produce a soft quality.

Time of Day: Midday sun creates harsh lighting and shadows. To avoid this, visit a waterfall at daybreak or an hour before sunset, and observe the wonderful quality of the light. Perhaps surprisingly, cloudy days are often better for waterfall photography, as they afford more photo opportunities.

Perspective: Waterfall photographs need a reference to indicate their size. To give a feeling of depth and space, use foreground elements, such as trees, rocks and people. In essence, try to frame the waterfall.

Position: Shoot from the top, bottom or side of the falls, but always try to keep one side of the image frame parallel to the ground. Basically, treat the waterfall like a piece of architecture. Be creative and see if you can photograph the falls from a unique, surprising perspective.

People: The high reflectance of water tends to underexpose people in a waterfall photograph. When positioning people, consider proper lighting for both them and the waterfall.

Rainbows: If you're lucky enough to find a rainbow at the end of a waterfall, take full advantage of it. Don't miss the opportunity for a spectacular photograph. Try photographing the rainbow and waterfall at different settings for a variety of looks.

Other Notes. Watch out for the sun. Light reflecting in the lens between the glass surfaces can cause a flare (diffused spot) or a ghost (a multisided bright spot). When it comes to the horizon line, it should be level and, in general, not placed in the center of the composition. Keep in mind that, if the sky isn't deep blue or contrasted by white clouds, it's fine to crop off the sky all together.

How to Use This Book

This book covers the entire state of Minnesota and is organized geographically. The state is divided into five regions: Southern, Metro, Boundary Waters Canoe Area Wilderness/Voyageurs National Park, From Sandstone to Duluth, and the North Shore. For an overview map with all of the falls, see page 12.

Within each region, the falls are ranked according to three general categories: Top 20, Must-See, and Other Falls. As you might expect, the Top 20 Falls are the best waterfalls the state has to offer, and these entries include four pages and a large photograph to show off these falls' beauty and power. The Must-See Falls are wonderful falls in their own right, as are the Other Falls, which only get shorter shrift because I didn't want this book to be 1,000 pages long. And if you just can't get enough, head to page 208 and you'll find a table with 24 More Waterfalls to Explore.

Of course, my rankings are subjective, and you may disagree with them. When it comes down to it, the state simply has too many wonderful waterfalls. That's a good problem, if you ask me!

In each section of the book, I include the following information for each waterfall:

Location: Where the waterfall is located; usually this is a park or other natural area. The approximate location is marked on the map to the left.

Address/GPS for the Falls: The street address of the falls, if possible. If that's not an option, the address for the park is listed. The GPS coordinates for the actual falls are also listed, though keep in mind that you can't drive right up to many falls. A short hike is often required, so don't plug this into the GPS of your car.

Directions: General driving directions to reach the falls.

Website: The website for the site if one exists.

Waterway: The river or stream that produces the falls; some falls, especially those in the BWCAW, are located along unnamed streams/rivers.

Nearest Town: The nearest town/city.

Height: The approximate height of the falls, though this can be difficult to measure for slowly sloping rapids.

Crest: The width of the falls; this can vary quite a bit depending on the season and rainfall patterns.

Hike Difficulty: How strenuous the hike is overall.

Trail Quality: How well marked and secure your footing is on the trail; often includes details about trail surface, obstacles and steps/stairs.

Round-trip Distance: The distance you'll need to hike from your car to the falls and back.

Admission: Some waterfalls are located in settings that charge admission. Fee information is listed here, as applicable.

Trip Report & Tips: A step-by-step account of my visit to the falls, including detailed directions to reach the falls and information about how to get a closer look, if you're feeling adventurous. Trip reports also include interesting sights and attractions to look out for on the way, possible hazards, recommended gear (think rain boots or bug spray), the best times to visit the falls and photograph them, as well as how accessible the trail is for those with disabilities.

Important Note: If you decide to get a closer look or scramble across slick rocks, be aware that this can be risky, especially if the water levels are high. So always use your discretion/judgment before heading off of the beaten path. When in doubt, enjoy the view from a distance.

A Note About Waterfall Names: In a few cases, the waterfalls I discuss in this book aren't officially named. To make things easier for the reader to follow, I've given the falls unofficial names. Of course, my nicknames for these falls are by no means definitive, so make up your own for each when you visit!

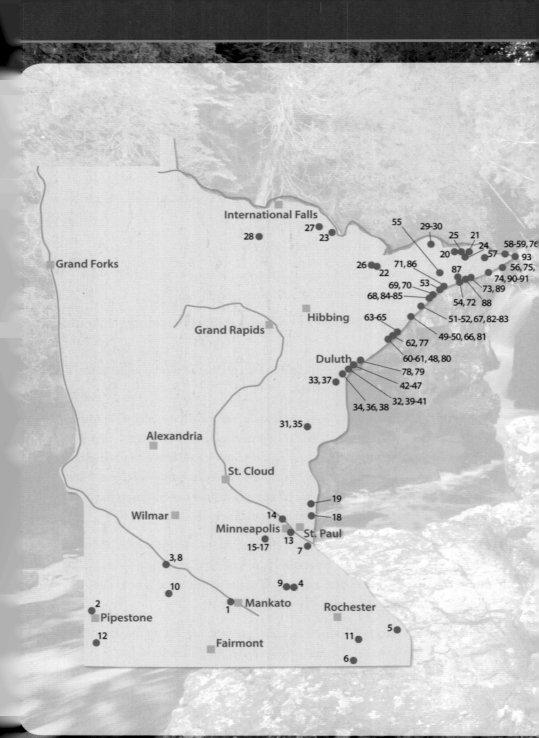

International Falls

Grand Forks

Hibbing

Grand Rapids

Duluth

Alexandria

St. Cloud

Wilmar

Minneapolis   St. Paul

Mankato

Rochester

Pipestone

Fairmont

55
29-30
27   25   21
28   23   20   24   58-59,76
26   71,86   57   93
22   87   56,75,
69,70   53   74,90-91
68,84-85   73,89
54,72   88
63-65   51-52,67,82-83
62,77   49-50,66,81
60-61,48,80
33,37   78,79
42-47
34,36,38   32,39-41

31,35

19
14   18
13
15-17
7

3,8
10
9   4
1

2
12   11
5
6

Map of Minnesota's Waterfalls

Southern Region
1. Minneopa Falls
2. Winnewissa Falls
3. Ramsey Falls
4. Hidden Falls
5. Pickwick Falls
6. Niagara Cave Falls
7. Vermillion Falls, Vermillion River
8. Redwood Falls
9. Caron Falls
10. Red Rock Falls
11. Root River Falls
12. Upper Mound Falls

Metro Region
13. Minnehaha Falls
14. St. Anthony Falls
15. Japanese Garden Waterfall
16. Woodland Waterfall
17. Waterfall Garden
18. Fairy Falls
19. Marine Mills Falls

BWCAW/Voyageurs NP/Surrounding Area
20. Bridal Falls
21. Johnson Falls
22. Kawishiwi Falls
23. Vermilion Falls
24. Crocodile Falls
25. Rose Lake Falls and Stairway Portage
26. Dry Falls
27. Ash River Falls
28. Big Falls
29. Upper Seagull Falls
30. Lower Seagull Falls

From Sandstone to Duluth Region
31. Wolf Creek Falls
32. Tischer Creek Falls
33. Swinging Bridge Falls and St. Louis Falls
34. Miller Creek Falls
35. Big Spring Falls
36. Kingsbury Creek Falls
37. Oldenburg Cascades
38. Blue Nude Falls
39. Chester Bowl Falls
40. Big Ten Falls
41. 4th Street Bridge Falls
42. Amity Creek Falls
43. Amity Falls at "The Deeps"
44. Keep Smiling Falls
45. Japp Hole Waterfall
46. Gunderson's Waterfall
47. The Shallows

The North Shore
48. Lower Gooseberry Falls
49. High Falls on the Baptism River
50. The Cascades on the Baptism River
51. Caribou Falls, Caribou River
52. The Cascades on the Manitou River
53. Onion River Falls
54. Cascade Falls on the Cascade River
55. Thompson Falls, Cascade River
56. Devil's Kettle, Brule River
57. Portage Brook Falls
58. Partridge Falls, Pigeon River
59. High Falls, Pigeon River
60. Upper Falls, Gooseberry River
61. Middle Falls, Gooseberry River
62. West Split Rock River Falls
63. Beaver River Falls
64. South Camp Falls, Beaver River
65. Glen Avon Falls, Beaver River
66. Illgen Falls, Baptism River
67. Mouth of the Manitou River
68. Upper Two Island River Falls
69. Cross River Falls, Upper and Lower
70. Seven Temperance River Falls
71. Lower Falls, Poplar River
72. The Cascades, Cascade River
73. Lower Falls, Fall River
74. Heart of the Earth Falls
75. Upper Falls on the Brule River
76. Upper and Lower Middle Falls, Pigeon River
77. Nine Falls on the Split Rock River
78. French River Falls
79. Train Trestle Falls
80. Fifth Falls, Gooseberry River
81. Two-Step Falls, Baptism River
82. Bridge Cascades on the Manitou River
83. Table Rock Falls, Manitou River
84. Two Island Falls, Two Island River
85. Triple Falls, Two Island River
86. Upper Falls and Cascades, Poplar River
87. Hidden Falls, Cascade River
88. Cut Face Creek Falls
89. Old Cedar Falls, Fall River
90. Colvill Falls
91. Tree-Hugger Falls, Kadunce River
92. Lower Falls, Brule River
93. Flute Reed River Falls

● Top 20   ● Must-See   ● Other

Minneopa Falls
Upper and Lower

Minneopa State Park was established in 1905 to preserve Minneopa Falls. The park and falls have been a popular visitor attraction since the 1850s.

There are actually two falls here: the main attraction, Minneopa Falls, with a height of 40 feet, and the Upper Falls, which are smaller, at only about 10 feet. Viewing the falls after heavy rains is a sure-fire way to see them in their full splendor.

Location: Minneopa State Park.

Address/GPS for the Falls: 54497 Gadwall Rd., Mankato, 56001; 44° 8'55.62" N, 94° 5'25.66" W.

Directions: 5 miles west of Mankato on MN-68 and U.S. Hwy. 169. Once at the state park, follow the waterfall signs to reach the falls.

Website: www.dnr.state.mn.us/state_parks/banning/index.html

Waterway: Minneopa Creek.

Height: Upper Falls are 10 feet; Minneopa Falls are 40 feet.

Crest: Varies.

Nearest Town: Mankato.

Hike Difficulty: Easy. **Trail Quality:** Fair.

Round-trip Distance: 0.3 mile to view from the top of the falls; 0.5 mile to view at river level and from the top walkway.

Admission: A day pass at the state park is $5. A yearly vehicle pass is $25 and allows you to enter all state parks for a year.

Trip Report & Tips: My girls and I really enjoyed visiting Minneopa Falls. Minneopa Creek flows atop soft sandstone; over time, it has gouged out the two waterfalls found here. The double waterfalls were created because the creek cut into the underlying sandstone layers at different rates. Between both falls, the water drops around 62 feet. (And sure enough, the word Minneopa means "falling water twice" in the Dakota language.)

Minneopa Falls is one of the largest waterfalls in southern Minnesota and one of the most picturesque. After just a short walk from the parking lot (300–500 feet), you will come up to the large gray bridge that crosses Minneopa Creek. On your left will be the Upper Falls, which can range from just a trickle to powerful falls. To reach Minneopa Falls, cross over the large pedestrian bridge and follow the paved path back to reach an overview above the falls. Keep going on the path to a limestone stairway. The 70 steps will bring you down to a wooden bridge crossing Minneopa Creek. There, you can walk back closer to Minneopa Falls on either side of the creek. We chose to not cross the bridge and instead captured an image with the river in the foreground and the falls in the background. If you head closer to the falls, keep in mind that the path back to the falls is not great, so wear footwear with good traction. Also, keep in mind that if you go on a day after heavy rainfall, the falls are going to be *loud*.

Winnewissa Falls

Winnewissa Falls is situated amid the sacred pipestone quarries at Pipestone National Monument. The falls, along with the surrounding quarries, are considered sacred by many American Indians.

Winnewissa Falls, Pipestone Creek

If you have kids in tow, have them stop by the visitor center to pick up a Junior Ranger activity booklet. If they complete the activities and return it to a ranger, they'll receive a Junior Ranger certificate and a badge. A Junior Birder program is available too!

Location: In the sacred pipestone quarries at Pipestone National Monument just north of the city of Pipestone.

Address/GPS for the Falls: 36 N Reservation Ave., Pipestone, 56164; 44° 0'54.95" N, 96° 19'14.44" W.

Directions: Located along Hwy. 75, Hwy. 23 and just north of Hwy. 30.

Website: www.nps.gov/pipe/

Waterway: Pipestone Creek.

Nearest Town: Pipestone.

Height: 15 feet. **Crest:** 12 feet.

Hike Difficulty: Easy. **Trail Quality:** Good.

Round-trip Distance: 0.75 mile.

Admission: $7 per person, ages 16 and up.

Trip Report & Tips: Our journey to Winnewissa Falls began on a rainy Saturday morning in June. With umbrellas in hand, we first headed up to the visitor center, which houses the Upper Midwest Indian Cultural Center. It's home to a gift shop, museum exhibits, a bookstore and a 22-minute film.

The quarries here have produced pipestone (also known as Catlinite) for thousands of years. The soft, malleable stone is used in ceremonial objects, especially pipes. Quarrying is limited to American Indians, but, during the summer months, American Indians sometimes lead cultural demonstrations where visitors can see pipestone carving in progress.

When you are ready to head to the waterfall, grab a trail map. You'll want to plan on a good hour for the 0.75-mile nature walk, which is known as the circle tour. On the paved trail, you'll stroll through the native tallgrass prairie and the pipestone quarries. You'll also pass by unique quartzite rock formations, such as Leaping Rock and Old Stone Face, as well as trail markers discussing the history of the area. You'll then pass over Pipestone Creek, and about halfway in you'll start to hear the falls. With the rocky creek in the foreground and the waterfall in the background, there are great photo opportunities along the way. As you near the falls, you can walk in front of them for great shots, and you can also climb up the chiseled stone steps around the falls. Since it was lightly raining on our visit, we had to be careful to avoid falling, but I'm actually glad everything was wet. It gave the red rocks added texture, and the images looked so much richer. After visiting the falls, you'll walk through some more of the interesting quarries as you circle back to the visitor center.

Ramsey Falls

Location: Alexander Ramsey Park.

Address/GPS for the Falls: 99 Oak St., Redwood Falls 56283; 44° 32'46.54" N, 95° 7'32.07" W.

Directions: In the heart of Redwood Falls.

Website: redwoodareacommunitycenter.com/area-parks/alexander-ramsey-park/

Waterway: Ramsey Creek.

Height: 45 feet. **Crest:** Varies.

Nearest Town: Redwood Falls.

Hike Difficulty: Easy. **Trail Quality:** Easy.

Round-trip Distance: Less than 0.1 mile.

Admission: None.

Trip Report & Tips: Nicknamed "Little Yellowstone of Minnesota," this is the largest municipal park in the state, covering 219 acres and featuring two waterfalls. As you drive down into the park, take a left before you cross the stone bridge and take a peek at the park's zoo, which has a nice variety of animals native to Minnesota. You'll see geese, ducks, bison, elk and deer, including an albino deer. After you've had your fill, get back in your vehicle, cross the bridge and head up the hill for 0.5 mile to the Ramsey Falls parking lot, where there's a short hike to the falls.

If you don't want to walk at all, go through the parking lot and turn right on the paved road, then go 0.2 mile farther and you can park right next to the falls. Head over to the lookout area for a high vantage point of the 45-foot falls. These falls aren't just relatively tall; they're also among the few waterfalls found in southern Minnesota. The park was originally built as a state park back in 1911; years later it was transferred back to the city of Redwood Falls. It has modern restrooms and shower facilities, 31 campsites, as well as a bevy of hiking trails, playgrounds and picnic areas—more than enough to keep you busy!

Location: Nerstrand Big Woods State Park.

Address/GPS for the Falls: 9700 170th St. E, Nerstrand, 55053; 44° 20'53.22" N, 93° 6'9.21" W.

Directions: Take I-35 to MN-19 east into Northfield. Go south on MN-3, east on MN-246, then turn south on Cty. Rd. 29 and follow the signs to the park entrance. It is approximately 11 miles southeast of Northfield.

Website: www.dnr.state.mn.us/state_parks/nerstrand_big_woods/index.html

Waterway: Prairie Creek.

Nearest Town: Northfield.

Height: 11 feet. **Crest:** 43 feet.

Hike Difficulty: Easy. **Trail Quality:** Good.

Round-trip Distance: 0.8 mile.

Admission: A day pass at the state park is $5. A yearly vehicle pass is $25 and allows you to enter all state parks for a year.

Trip Report & Tips: On a very mild March afternoon I decided to head down to Nerstrand Big Woods State Park to find Hidden Falls. My daughter Nora was along for the ride and so was her friend Rachel. We parked in the spacious parking lot near the picnic area and put on our winter clothes and boots. As you head across the picnic area, watch for signage for Hidden Falls. You'll be turning left and heading downhill for 0.3 mile. Watch for signage along the way with information about the history of the park and the falls. As we strolled over the snow-covered boardwalk down to the bridge at the falls area, everything was totally frozen and very slick. We decided to (carefully) venture out on the clear ice. It was very quiet and we couldn't hear any running water beneath the ice. We were able to walk right along the edge of the falls, examining the huge frozen icicles. The falls are 10 feet high in the summertime but only about 6 feet high when frozen. The frozen falls are really a must-see, as they look beautiful when draped in ice.

Location: Pickwick Mill.

Address/GPS for the Falls: 24813 Cty. Rd. 7, Winona, 55987; 43° 58'50.07" N, 91° 29'45.80" W.

Directions: Heading from the Holiday Inn Express in Winona, travel 8 miles southeast on Hwy. 61. Go southwest 1.9 miles on Cty. Rd. 7 into Pickwick. The mill will be on your right-hand side and it will be hard to miss; Pickwick is a tiny town.

Website: www.pickwickmill.org

Waterway: Big Trout Creek.

Height: 16 feet. **Crest:** Varies.

Nearest Town: Pickwick.

Hike Difficulty: Easy. **Trail Quality:** Fair.

Round-trip Distance: 0.2 mile.

Admission: None; the mill is open seasonally; check online for hours.

Trip Report & Tips: Park at the mill's parking lot. Just off of Cty. Rd. 7, you'll find two paths going down to the falls. One is steep, so you'll want to hang onto some trees on your way down. The other path has makeshift steps, as well as a rope that you'll need to hang onto on your way down. As you are down near the pond area, take time to admire the tall yellow limestone walls. Look closely at the water flowing over the stone ledge, and you'll see how the creek cuts back at the limestone layer, forming the falls. To explore the mill, you can take the little, well-worn path from the mill parking lot and head over to the dam and Big Trout Creek. The six-story limestone mill was built from 1856 to 1858 by Thomas Grant and Wilson Davis. It was originally built as a sawmill and later converted into a gristmill. During the Civil War, it ran 24 hours a day, producing 100 barrels of flour a day for the Union Army. The mill is powered by a 20-foot water wheel, and if you tour it you'll see that most of the original machinery is still in place and some is even operable. The mill and waterfall are beautiful at any time of year, but they are especially scenic in the fall.

Location: Niagara Cave Falls is located inside Niagara Cave, just south of Harmony.

Address/GPS for the Falls: 29842 Cty. Rd. 30, Harmony, 55939; 43° 30'50.76" N, 92° 3'18.14" W.

Directions: From Harmony, go 2.5 miles south on MN-139 and 2.3 miles west on Cty. Rd. 30; watch for signs leading you to the cave.

Website: www.niagaracave.com

Waterway: The source of the falls is known only as the "underground stream." It comes out at Hawkeye Springs on the banks of the Upper Sioux River.

Nearest Town: Harmony.

Height: The main falls are 50 feet high, with the stream working its way down 10 feet prior to the big drop. **Crest:** Varies by season.

Hike Difficulty: Easy once you're down into the cave, but there are around 250 steps to tackle to get there. Given the distance, be sure to wear good walking shoes or tennis shoes, warm clothes (the cave is a constant 48 degrees) and some type of hat, as you'll likely get dripped on. Note: There are no bats in this cave.

Trail Quality: Good.

Round-trip Distance: 0.8 mile.

Admission: $14 for adults; $8 for kids.

Trip Report & Tips: Niagara Cave is one of my favorite Minnesota tours; it's an hour long, informative and just plain amazing. You'll see the magnificent waterfall at your very first stop at the bottom of the steps. After admiring the falls, follow your informative guide through the twists and turns of the cave and learn all about the history of the cave. The cave is full of stalactites, stalagmites and a wide array of colorful minerals. Oddly, the cave was only discovered by accident, when three pigs went missing back in 1924. The pigs were found, alive, and the farm boys who found them also discovered the twisting passages of the cave, which quickly became a tourist destination.

Location: In Vermillion Falls Park and near the Ramsey Mill Ruins.

Address/GPS for the Falls: Located off Hwy. 61 and 21st St. E, Hastings, 55033; 44° 43'32.10" N, 92° 50'41.76" W.

Directions: If you are heading south on Hwy. 61, you'll want to turn left after the ConAgra Flour Mill onto 21st St. E, and the park will be on your left.

Website: www.hastingsmn.gov/city-government/city-departments/parks-recreation

Waterway: Vermillion River.

Nearest Town: Hastings.

Height: The Main Falls are approximately 45 feet high; the Upper Falls are 8 feet high.

Crest: Approximately 35–45 feet.

Hike Difficulty: Easy. **Trail Quality:** Good, short paved trail.

Round-trip Distance: 0.1 mile.

Admission: None.

Trip Report & Tips: From the parking lot, it's a short and easy walk to the covered gazebo for your first look at Vermillion Falls. Walk down the paved path to find a more scenic view than the fenced-in overlooks. Here you'll see—and hear—the very loud falls as the water plummets deep into the gorge. If you head farther down, you'll find a pedestrian bridge crossing over the gorge that will lead you to Old Mill Park. Looking at the falls, they first flow over a man-made cement ledge that's about 6–8 feet high. You can get very close to the short falls and actually sit on the ledge. The water then glides over the surface for a bit and plunges down a good 35–45 feet as it hits the rocky river floor. In the nineteenth and early twentieth centuries, the river was used for water power for area gristmills; one was even built by Alexander Ramsey, Minnesota's first governor. The area's milling ties continue to this day: To the north of the river is the massive ConAgra flour mill.

Redwood Falls

Location: Alexander Ramsey Park.

Address/GPS for the Falls: 99 Oak St., Redwood Falls 56283; 44° 32'35.89" N, 95° 7'9.77" W.

Directions: Redwood Falls is located 0.2 mile southeast from Ramsey Falls. To get there, follow Cty. Rd. 31 southeast from the Ramsey Falls lot. The road will twist and turn a bunch; stay to the right, and park at the Zeb Gray playground.

Website: www.redwoodareacommunitycenter.com

Waterway: Redwood River.

Height: 14-16 feet. **Crest:** Varies.

Nearest Town: Redwood Falls.

Hike Difficulty: Moderate. **Trail Quality:** Good; paved path down to the bridge.

Round-trip Distance: 0.2 mile.

Admission: None.

Trip Report & Tips: With the playground in front of you, you'll be facing southeast; head past the playground and down a steep paved path. A two-minute walk leads you to a bench and a skinny brown pedestrian bridge going over the falls. My girls and I crossed the bridge, took a left and carefully stepped and slid down the huge rocks alongside the river. We chose to go on a day after some fresh March snow. You'll be able to get some great panoramic images if you stand up on the huge rocks alongside the river. My girls and I all agreed this was a much more fun falls to visit compared to Ramsey Falls, just because it was more adventurous and challenging. The city of Redwood Falls has owned and operated its own electrical power company since 1946; the falls you see here actually power a dam that provides backup power for the city.

Caron Falls

Location: Caron Park.

Address/GPS for the Falls: 6816 170th St. E, Faribault 55021; 44° 20'59.56" N, 93° 9'55.79" W.

Directions: Located north of Cty. Rd. 88 (170th St.) and 3 miles from Nerstrand Big Woods State Park.

Website: www.co.rice.mn.us/node/2020

Waterway: Prairie Creek.

Nearest Town: Faribault.

Height: 5.5 feet. **Crest:** 17 feet.

Hike Difficulty: Easy. **Trail Quality:** Good.

Round-trip Distance: 0.6 mile.

Admission: None.

Trip Report & Tips: Park in the parking lot and pass by the picnic shelter, heading to the northwest corner of the grassy area. Take the path and start gradually heading downhill for 0.3 mile. Follow the trail until you hear the waterfall, then veer off the path on your left. There you'll see that there are actually two waterfalls present. The second smaller falls are about 5 feet high and 4 feet wide. They gracefully fall over little rock ledges chiseled out of limestone. Over at the main falls, you'll find a very unique V-shaped limestone chunk that the water flows over. Head up on top of the falls and hike along the streambed, where you'll find an impressive steel footbridge. All in all, the park is very kid friendly; best of all, the hike to the falls only takes 10 minutes.

Note: Bring bug spray, wear rain boots and be aware that the primitive bathrooms on site may not be available (they weren't when we visited!).

Red Rock Falls

Location: Red Rock Falls County Park.

Address/GPS for the Falls: 48771 250th St., Sanborn, 56083; 44° 7'17.97" N, 95° 6'17.76" W.

Directions: From Windom, take Hwy. 71 north to Cty. Rd. 10 east and turn right. Then turn left on the very first gravel road you encounter; it's 460th Ave., and you'll head north. Go exactly 1 mile and turn left on an unmarked gravel road. The park will be down a little bit on your left.

Website: www.co.cottonwood.mn.us/county-departments/parks/county-parks/

Waterway: Mound Creek.

Nearest Town: Sanborn.

Height: 30 feet. **Crest:** 1–3 feet.

Hike Difficulty: Easy.

Trail Quality: Good; the trail consists of mowed grass.

Round-trip Distance: Less than 0.1 mile.

Admission: None.

Trip Report & Tips: From the parking area, head right across the lawn, and then down the path. Listen for the waterfall and let your feet lead you to it. Nora and I walked back, around and down into the dells area. The tall, skinny falls flow down gently into a large shallow pool in the gorge area. When we were visiting, kids were swimming in the water east of the falls, squealing and having fun.

On our visit, we climbed up on a huge rock in front of the falls. Climbing on top of the rock gives you the best view of the gorge and the Red Rock Dells.

When you visit, stop over to see the ancient Jeffers Petroglyphs, which are just 4 miles away. To get there, go east 2 miles on Cty. Rd. 10 and then south 1 mile on Cty. Rd. 2.

Root River Falls

Location: Located on the Root River in Lanesboro.

Address/GPS for the Falls: 43° 43'0.39" N, 91° 58'44.27" W.

Directions: From Lanesboro, you'll want to get on Parkway Ave. S; it's hard to miss because Parkway Ave. is Lanesboro's main street. Follow Parkway Ave. S until you reach Kirkwood St. W. Take a right, and park on the side of the road.

Website: www.lanesboro.com

Waterway: Root River.

Nearest Town: Lanesboro.

Height: 26 feet. **Crest:** The dam is 150 feet wide.

Hike Difficulty: Easy. **Trail Quality:** Good.

Round-trip Distance: 0.1 mile.

Admission: None.

Trip Report & Tips: From your street-side parking lot, head to the end of the road, where you'll find a path down to the river. The stone dam was built in 1868 and has provided hydroelectric power to the town of Lanesboro ever since. The dam is built out of 2.5-inch-thick limestone blocks, and its maximum discharge is 16,700 cubic feet per second. Lanesboro's dam and hydro plant are among the oldest still-operating hydroelectric plants in the country.

For another scenic view of the dam waterfall, head up to the top of the hill in town. Here you can get a bird's-eye view of the falls, and you'll be guaranteed a beautiful view of the city in any season.

Upper Mound Falls

Location: Blue Mounds State Park.

Address/GPS for the Falls: 1410 161st St., Luverne, 56156; 43° 43'5.59" N, 96° 11'24.84" W.

Directions: From Luverne, go north 4 miles on MN-75. Turn east on Cty. Rd. 20 and go 1 mile to the park entrance.

Website: www.dnr.state.mn.us/state_parks/blue_mounds

Waterway: Mound Creek.

Height: 7 feet. **Crest:** 45 feet.

Nearest Town: Luverne.

Hike Difficulty: Easy.

Trail Quality: There are nice mowed paths on the west side of the falls and you can park in the amphitheater parking lot. If you hike down from the south side campsites, you'll be hiking through very tall grass with no real path. You'll also have to hop over the creek and climb some rocks, but it's doable.

Round-trip Distance: From the amphitheater parking lot on the west side, it's 0.2 mile. From the south side campsite parking lot, it's 0.4 mile.

Admission: A day pass at the state park is $5. A yearly vehicle pass is $25 and allows you to enter all state parks for a year.

Trip Report & Tips: Once in the park, you'll pass by the small information office. After the office building, you're going to want to take a left. Head down the road and you'll see the waterfall off to your right. If you want to take the easy way down, park in the amphitheater parking lot by the campgrounds and follow the mowed path back to the falls area. If you want more adventure, park in the campground parking lot just to the south of the falls, put your boots on and head through the tall grass, burnweed and across the rocks.

Once you actually cross over the creek, you can get much closer to the huge rocks located by the falls. As you'll notice, this waterfall is actually a dam that was built in 1937. The dam is listed on the National Register of Historic Places.

Minnehaha Falls

Minnehaha Park

A Minnesota landmark,
Minnehaha Falls has been
revered by countless generations.

Located in the heart of the Twin Cities, Minnehaha is the perfect place to get away from the workaday world.

Location: South Minneapolis in Minnehaha Park.

Address/GPS for the Falls: 4801 S Minnehaha Dr., Minneapolis 55417; 44° 54'55.23" N, 93° 12'39.30" W.

Directions: Located in the heart of the metro area, there are many different ways to get here.

Website: www.nps.gov/miss/planyourvisit/minnehah.htm

Waterway: Minnehaha Creek.

Nearest Town: Minneapolis.

Height: 53 feet. **Crest:** 20 feet.

Hike Difficulty: Easy (paved path, handicapped accessible on the top).

Trail Quality: Good. A bridge crosses the falls, and it features a paved trail. If you want to descend to the river level, you'll need to take the stairs. On the north side, there are 107 steps down to the bottom of the falls. On the south side, there are 113 steps to the bottom. There are also 87 steps to reach the south-side lookout.

Round-trip Distance: 0.4 mile.

Admission: None.

Trip Report & Tips: If you want a comfortable stroll, there are accessible paved trails on the bridge that goes over the top of this urban waterfall. If you want to venture down to the base of the falls, it takes a bit more work, as you'll need to head down more than 100 steps, where you will find another bridge down at the river level. There you can view the falls from both sides of the river. The park also boasts many statues and sculptures. (Also, before you begin your hike, don't forget to pay for parking; I don't know of any free parking in the area.)

The Falls get their name from Henry Wadsworth Longfellow's famous poem, "The Song of Hiawatha." The story recounts the tale of another name familiar to Minnesotans, Hiawatha, and his love, Minnehaha. Despite Longfellow's influence on the Twin Cities—there's even a neighborhood named after him—Longfellow never actually visited Minnesota.

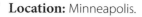

Location: Minneapolis.

Address/GPS for the Falls: Mill Ruins Park, 130 Portland Ave S, Minneapolis, 55401; 44° 58'54.69" N, 93° 15'25.45" W.

Directions: I usually park on S 2nd St. next to the Mill City Museum. Note: You'll need to pay for parking on the streets.

If you park on S 2nd St., either go through the Mill City Museum or walk down 2nd St. and take a right onto Portland Ave. This will bring you down to the Mill Ruins Park and the Stone Arch Bridge. Walk across the bridge to view the falls.

Website: www.nps.gov/miss/planyourvisit/stanfall.htm

Waterway: Mississippi River.

Height: 49 feet. **Crest:** 1,575 feet overall; the longest continuous structure is 416 feet long.

Nearest Town: Minneapolis.

Hike Difficulty: Easy. **Trail Quality:** Good.

Round-trip Distance: 0.6 mile.

Admission: None.

Trip Report & Tips: These are the falls that started it all. Once a wild waterfall that was perhaps 20 feet tall, St. Anthony Falls was revered by the Dakota Indians. After settlement, the falls became the primary source of power for Minneapolis and its nascent flour milling industry. So many mills sprang up that Minneapolis was dubbed the Mill City, but by the 1860s, all the activity on the river accelerated the falls' natural retreat, and this in turn began to compromise the structural integrity of the actual falls. This threat came to a head in 1869, when a portion of the river floor collapsed due to construction of a tunnel under the river. This disaster made a complete collapse of the falls (and the end of their use to industry) a real possibility. Eventually, a wooden scaffolding was built to protect the falls, followed by the concrete curtain that still exists today. More than a century later, the falls are still producing power; a dam owned and operated by Xcel Energy produces 12 megawatts of power.

Japanese Garden Waterfall

Location: Minnesota Landscape Arboretum.

Address/GPS for the Falls: 3675 Arboretum Dr., Chaska 55318; 44° 51'43.38" N, 93° 37'2.59" W.

Directions: 4 miles west of Chanhassen.

Website: www.arboretum.umn.edu

Waterway: Unnamed stream.

Height: The Upper Falls are 6 feet high; the Lower Falls are 9 feet high.

Crest: 4 feet.

Nearest Town: Chaska.

Hike Difficulty: Easy. **Trail Quality:** Good.

Round-trip Distance: 0.2 mile.

Admission: $13 for ages 13 and up. Under 13 free. No admission on certain Thursdays.

Trip Report & Tips: Drive in at the main entrance and park. Your visit should start at the Oswald Visitor Center. There you'll find an information booth where you can pick up a map and purchase a ticket for a very informative 45-minute (seasonal) tram ride around the beautifully landscaped grounds. There is also a nice big gift shop, a cafe and a library. To find the waterfall, head out one of the back doors and pass through the Rose Walk. The Japanese Garden will be across the road to your right. Find the very secluded area and head under the thatched roof arbor. The welcoming waterfall will be off to your left. This beautifully secluded waterfall is man-made and surrounded by a tranquil Koi pond. The garden reflects a style of Japanese gardens from the Edo Period (1609–1869). The garden was built around the concept of "reveal and conceal," so when you visit, you will never be able to see everything at once. You must move around in nature's beauty, take time to reflect and explore the many different areas within the Japanese Garden.

Woodland Waterfall

Location: Minnesota Landscape Arboretum.

Address/GPS for the Falls: 3675 Arboretum Dr., Chaska 55318; 44° 51'41.65" N, 93° 37'6.60" W.

Directions: 4 miles west of Chanhassen.

Website: www.arboretum.umn.edu

Waterway: Unnamed stream.

Height: The Upper Falls are 6 feet, the Lower Falls are 3 feet.

Crest: Varies.

Nearest Town: Chaska.

Hike Difficulty: Easy. **Trail Quality:** Good.

Round-trip Distance: 0.3 mile.

Admission: $13 for ages 13 and up. Under 13 free. No admission on certain Thursdays.

Trip Report & Tips: From the Japanese Garden, head either through the Hosta Glade area (which has over 300 varieties of hostas) or around the Home Demo Gardens back to the Woodland Azalea Garden. Here you'll find the top of the waterfall backing up against the paved 3-mile loop trail shared by cars, bikes and pedestrians. This waterfall has a 6-foot top level that flows down over the black slate stone, under the stone pathway and then flows down 3 more feet into a large Koi pond. This waterfall area is in a more open space than the very secluded Japanese Garden. Around the waterfall you'll find a variety of plants, including native winterberry, the northern lights series of azaleas and butterbur, which has the largest leaves of any garden perennial. In all, the arboretum is home to 3 beautifully landscaped waterfall areas; all are within walking distance of the Oswald Visitor Center and most are somewhat handicapped accessible.

Waterfall Garden

Location: Minnesota Landscape Arboretum.

Address/GPS for the Falls: 3675 Arboretum Dr., Chaska 55318; 44° 51'39.48" N, 93° 36'56.53" W.

Directions: 4 miles west of Chanhassen.

Website: www.arboretum.umn.edu

Waterway: Unnamed stream.

Height: See trip report for details. **Crest:** Varies.

Nearest Town: Chaska.

Hike Difficulty: Easy. **Trail Quality:** Good.

Round-trip Distance: 0.2 mile.

Admission: $13 for ages 13 and up. Under 13 free. No admission on certain Thursdays.

Trip Report & Tips: Out of the three waterfall areas at the landscape arboretum, this one is my favorite. To get there, exit out of the front door closest to the gift shop of the Oswald Visitor Center and take an immediate right. Walk across the Welcoming Terrace and back to the Terrace Garden. Take a right and you'll enter the Waterfall Garden, which is beautifully landscaped and has 5 easy-going waterfalls. The Upper Falls are easy to find, as it's right next to the sidewalk. It starts down at about 2 feet then rolls across boulders as it nears the walkway and goes down another 4 feet. If you step back into the conifer area and go to the wooden platform, you'll see the second falls flowing down about 3 feet among some large boulders. Then, head down and around to the third falls, the shaded 10-foot falls. If you keep following the path, you'll find the fourth falls. They drop about 6 feet under the footbridge; to view the fifth falls, head to the bottom of the hill, where you'll find small, graceful falls that are 4 feet high and 5 feet wide. Note: Getting down to the bottom is tricky, so use caution.

Fairy Falls

Location: Stillwater.

Address/GPS for the Falls: Located near Fairy Falls Rd. 45° 4'52.95" N, 92° 48'25.55" W.

Directions: From Stillwater, drive north on Hwy. 95 1.1 miles to the intersection of Hwy. 95 and Hwy. 96. Turn left and head west on Hwy. 96, and go about 0.1 mile and take an immediate right onto Cty. Rd. 11 (also known as Boom Rd.). Proceed for 0.2 mile, turn left and head up Fairy Falls Rd. for 0.2 mile. Turn left onto Orwell Ave. and park on the right side of the road. You'll see the worn shoulder where everyone parks.

Website: None.

Waterway: Silver Creek.

Height: 27 feet. **Crest:** 2–6 feet.

Nearest Town: Stillwater.

Hike Difficulty: Steep and strenuous.

Trail Quality: Rough; wear waterproof hiking boots.

Round-trip Distance: The hike down the steep hill to the top of the falls and back up the hill to your car is about 0.1 mile or 0.2 mile, if you head to the bottom of the falls.

Admission: None.

Trip Report & Tips: To hike down to the falls, cross Fairy Falls Rd. and head down a steep, short path to the wooden footbridge. You'll find yourself at the top of the falls. If you want a shortcut, turn right before you get to the bridge. Take the little path that leads you to about a 25-foot climb straight down. If you're brave, you can use the rocks as stepping stones to carefully venture to the canyon floor. When you get to the creek, there will be logs and rocks to scramble over. Your feet might get wet and your knees may get muddy, depending on how much you want to explore.

Marine Mills Falls

Location: Marine on St. Croix.

Address/GPS for the Falls: The falls are located directly across from the Security State Bank of Marine at 120 Judd St., Marine on St. Croix, 55047; 45° 11'53.35" N, 92° 46'9.25" W.

Directions: Located 12 miles north of Stillwater and 15 miles south of Taylors Falls on MN-95.

Website: www.marineonstcroix.org

Waterway: St. Croix River.

Height: Cascades down 16 feet. **Crest:** 6 feet.

Nearest Town: Marine on St. Croix.

Hike Difficulty: Easy.

Trail Quality: Good up on street level. There are also paths around the old sawmill area and nice signage put up by the Minnesota Historical Society.

Round-trip Distance: 0.1 mile.

Admission: None.

Trip Report & Tips: The falls are located right in the center of town and spill out of a tunnel on Judd St. The history of the falls is intertwined with the Marine Lumber Company, which operated from 1839–1895 and was Minnesota's first commercial sawmill. Today, the old mill is largely gone, but plan on spending some time exploring this fun little historic town. They have a library/town hall built in 1888, and an awesome general store built in 1870 and filled with groceries, gift items and tasty baked goods. The Mill area itself is well worth a tour. After sitting vacant for many years, the mill site was protected, thanks to the efforts of a group of history-minded residents. The site is now listed on the National Register of Historic Places.

Bridal Falls

BWCAW

A graceful, intricate falls, Bridal Falls is well-deserving of its poetic name.

BWCAW/VOYAGEURS NP/ SURROUNDING AREA

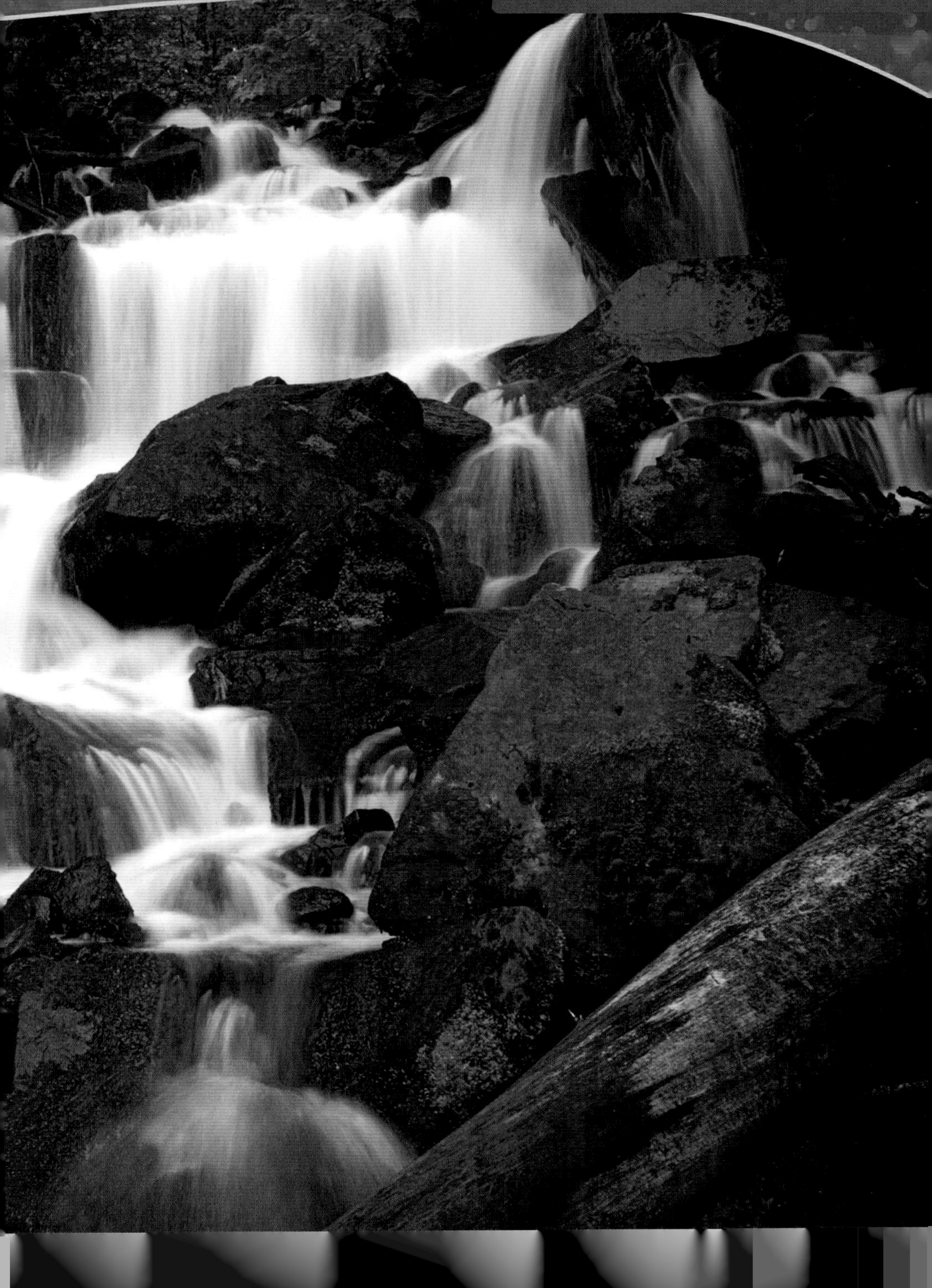

This is a great place to visit on a really hot day. Just stand with your back to the falls and feel the refreshing mist flow over you.

Location: On the Gunflint Trail.

Address/GPS for the Falls: The southeast corner of Gunflint Lake; 48° 5'29.69" N, 90° 38'5.62" W.

Directions: Near Gunflint Lodge and accessible by boat or a short hike. (If you're taking a boat, note that Gunflint Lake can be very choppy if it's windy.)

Website: None.

Waterway: Unnamed stream that flows from Crab Lake and empties into Gunflint Lake.

Nearest Town: Grand Marais.

Height: 25 feet. **Crest:** 70 feet.

Hike Difficulty: Easy, on the hike back to the falls. Once you're at the falls area, it can be strenuous since you're climbing a steep pile of slippery, jagged rocks.

Trail Quality: Moderate; there are lots of rocks and roots to step over; also, the trail can be very wet, so you may want to wear waterproof boots.

Round-trip Distance: 0.8 mile; the path generally follows the stream back to the falls. As you near Bridal Falls, the stream gets wider and picks up speed.

Trip Report & Tips: Bridal Falls is one of the most unique waterfalls in the entire state, and it's one of my all-time favorites. The falls actually consist of two really distinct waterfalls. The falls on the right-hand side resemble a white lacy bridal veil flowing down and give the falls their name. The falls on the left look like your typical Boundary Waters waterfall, a torrent of water racing down over black, jagged rocks. As a whole, the area is so unique because the mist that the falls produce rains back down on the rocks, allowing trees to grow almost on the bare rock. The end result is stunning; instead of Bridal Falls, the name Fairy Tale Falls is almost more appropriate because you truly get that sense when visiting the falls, which are surrounded by moss-covered rocks that are situated in a verdant, wooded area.

When you're exploring around the falls area, be very careful and wear high-traction footwear or boots. If you head up for a closer look at the falls, you'll be climbing in some steep, rocky areas, so use extreme caution. As you climb up to the falls on the left, you'll see that they are about 6–12 feet wide, and at the top, the falls drop around 16 dramatic feet and then they rapidly rush down another 50 feet or so with many drops along the way.

Perhaps surprisingly, the waterfalls face north, and the water from the falls flows north to Hudson Bay.

Johnson Falls

BWCAW

A secluded series of three falls is located in the Boundary Waters Canoe Area Wilderness. Seeing these waterfalls takes some effort. But it's well worth it!

BWCAW/VOYAGEURS NP/ SURROUNDING AREA

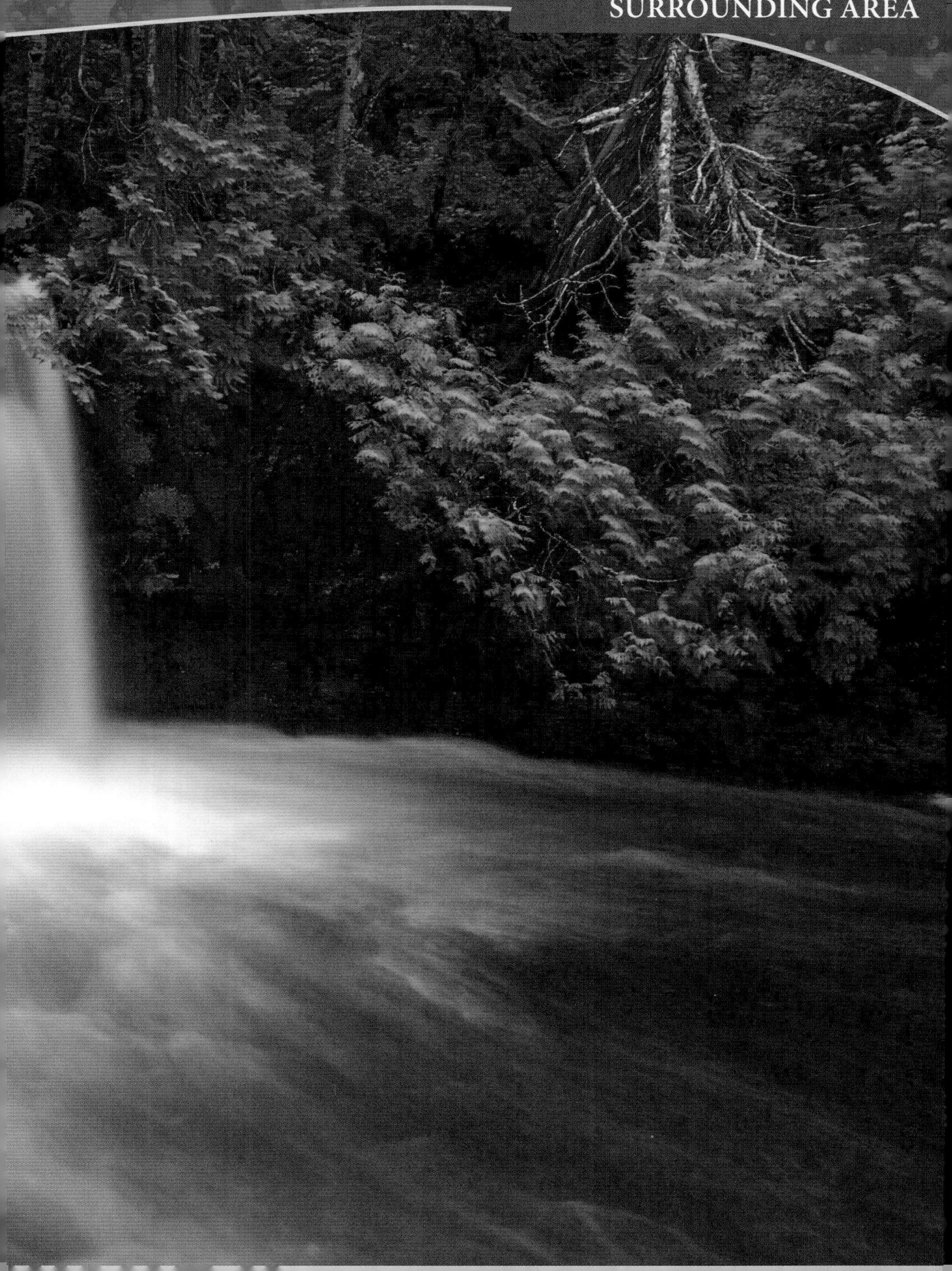

Johnson Falls is one of the most impressive waterfalls in the Boundary Waters. It consists of three separate waterfalls; each is unique, and they are certainly worth the strenuous hike to view them.

Location: A 0.5-mile hike from the west end of Pine Lake.

Address/GPS for the Falls: 48° 3'40.52" N, 90° 15'47.38" W.

Directions: Unless you've been here before, it's best to hire a guide.

Website: None.

Waterway: Unnamed river running from Rocky Lake to Pine Lake.

Nearest Town: Grand Marais.

Height: Lower Falls are 25 feet high; the Upper Falls are about 25–30 feet high.

Crest: The Lower Falls have a crest of about 30 feet; the Upper Falls have a crest of about 20 feet.

Hike Difficulty: Moderate to strenuous.

Trail Quality: Fair.

Round-trip Distance: More than 10 miles. See description below.

Admission: Fees vary by guide service.

Trip Report & Tips: I'm glad I photographed these falls, but I'm also glad it's over! We headed out from Bearskin Lodge on a peaceful, calm and overcast morning with Quinn, our awesome guide. We paddled on East Bearskin Lake for 3.5 miles from Bearskin Lodge. Our first portage was a short and easy one, hiking northeast to Alder Lake, where we paddled another 2 peaceful miles. Then it was time for another short portage, this time to Canoe Lake, where we enjoyed an easy 0.75-mile paddle.

We reached our final portage site, a steep 0.7-mile portage that can be one of the more grueling ones in the Boundary Waters. The first 0.1 mile is an uphill climb with some stone steps and rocks; the next 0.6 mile rises and falls, and there are rocks, roots and fallen trees to watch out for. (Thankfully, you can leave your canoe and gear at the start of the portage, as you'll just be hiking to the falls.) After a couple of turns, you will see Pine Lake in front of you; hang a left and walk alongside the lake for a while. There are a number of trails to choose from, but they are often muddy and sloppy. (This is where we saw moose tracks and scat but no moose.) As you rise again in elevation, the path will turn to the left and wrap around a densely wooded cliff area. Be careful: You'll be up high and the stream will be down below on your right. By this point, the noise of the falls will be apparent, and once you come around the corner you'll see the lower set of Johnson Falls before you. Be sure to explore all the many nooks and crannies in this area. Once you're satisfied with the lower set of falls, find a trail and head up to the middle falls and the rocky cascading rapids area—again, very picturesque. (That's where I lost my tripod, though thankfully my camera wasn't on it!) After that, continue to the top of the Upper Falls area. Don't forget to save enough time for the journey (and paddle) back. Our hike back to the canoe took us 40 minutes. The 0.7-mile portage trail stretch is definitely more uphill on the way back, so have an energy snack while you are at the falls area and save some water for the hike (and paddle) back.

Kawishiwi Falls

Edge of BWCAW

A source of hydroelectric power for nearly a century, Kawishiwi Falls is a massive waterfall just a few miles from Ely.

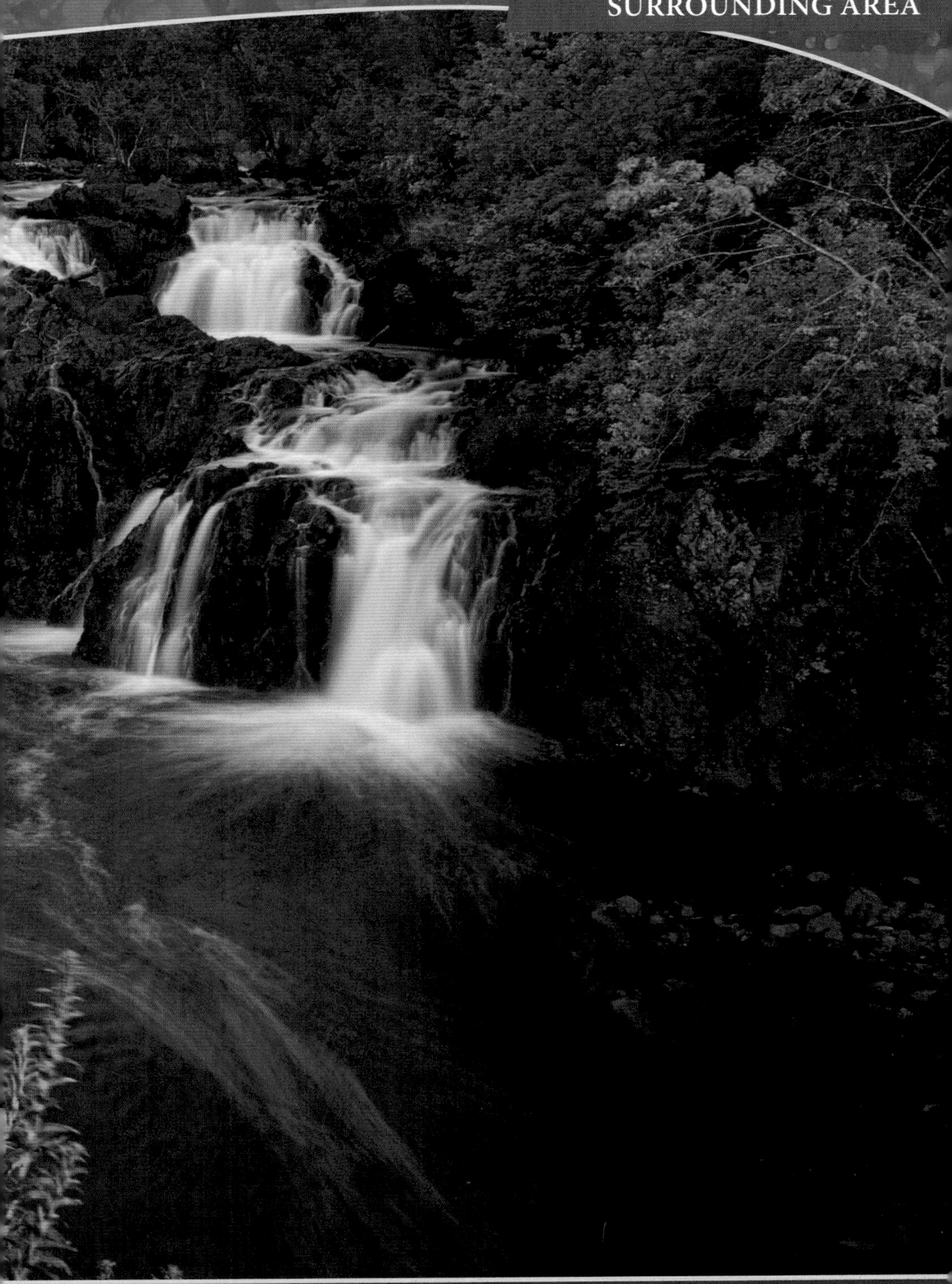

Kawishiwi Falls, Kawishiwi River

Located on the very edge of the Boundary Waters Canoe Area Wilderness, Kawishiwi Falls tumbles down 71 feet into Fall Lake.

Location: On the edge of the Boundary Waters Canoe Area Wilderness.

Address/GPS for the Falls: 4.5 miles east of Ely; 47° 56'2.53" N, 91° 45'43.49" W.

Directions: From Ely, go 4.5 miles east on U.S. Hwy. 169. After driving past the small town of Winton, 169 turns into Fernberg Rd. Keep heading east; you'll go over a bridge as you pass by Garden Lake. Just as you see the Deer Ridge Resort sign on your right (their address is 444 Fernberg Rd.) you'll take an immediate left and park in the parking lot.

Website: None.

Waterway: Kawishiwi River, located between Fall Lake and Garden Lake.

Nearest Town: Winton.

Height: 71 feet. **Crest:** 140 feet.

Hike Difficulty: Easy. **Trail Quality:** Fair.

Round-trip Distance: 0.7 mile.

Admission: None.

Trip Report & Tips: Look for the Kawishiwi Falls map at the entrance to the wooded trail. The path is a bit uneven and crosses over lots of roots, rocks and boardwalks, so wear good hiking shoes. You'll see lots of birch trees with wild roots along the way. At 0.2 mile in, take the trail to the right (the trail makes a loop). As you get closer to the falls area you'll hear the thunder of the falls. After 0.4 mile you'll be in front of the spectacular falls. They flow to the north and then take a 90-degree turn and head into Fall Lake.

This trail didn't open to the public until May 2006, so before then, this was a secret place. Even many local Ely residents didn't know about the massive waterfall in their own backyard. While you're enjoying the view, have fun exploring, but be wary of the steep cliffs at the observation points. One lookout point has a bench and some informational signage about the falls, which power the adjacent Falls Lake hydroelectric dam. Prior to their use for power, the falls were an obstacle that American Indians, explorers and voyageurs had to portage around, though, by the late 1800s, the falls were also used to send lumber downstream to the town of Winton.

On our visit, my girls and I spent 50 minutes at the falls viewing area while the sun was setting on a beautiful July evening. Our return hike to the parking lot took us only eight minutes.

Location: South of Crane Lake on the Vermilion River.

Address/GPS for the Falls: 48° 15'43.65" N, 92° 34'16.48" W.

Directions: From Buyck, take Cty. Rd. 24 north to Forest Rd. 491, then turn left and drive 5.25 miles, then cross over the Vermilion River. Continue 0.2 mile and turn left into Vermilion Falls Recreation Area and park there. From the recreation area parking lot, follow the handicap-accessible trail approximately 0.1 mile to the overlook.

Website: Located in Superior National Forest, www.fs.usda.gov/superior

Waterway: Vermilion River.

Height: The falls and rapids cover about 25 feet as they flow down a huge slope.

Crest: Varies.

Nearest Town: Crane Lake.

Hike Difficulty: Easy. **Trail Quality:** Good.

Round-trip Distance: 0.25 mile.

Admission: None.

Trip Report & Tips: With just a short hike, these are very easy falls to reach, and they're also accessible for those with disabilities. This also can be a fairly busy place. My daughters and I went on July 6th. It was a heavily overcast day with light sprinkles, but the place was still very busy; crowds are not something we waterfallers are used to, given how often we have sites to ourselves. So to avoid the crowds, I'd recommend heading to the falls either early in the day or toward the evening. I'd also avoid peak viewing weekends, such as the Fourth of July.

Getting to the falls is easy enough; after a short hike you'll come up to a long wooden boardwalk and the large observation deck, practically guaranteeing you a good viewing spot. When my girls and I visited in July, the water levels were high and the Vermilion River was raging through the narrow gorge. Also consider checking out the rest of the river, which has many impressive rapids.

Location: Southern shore of East Bearskin Lake in the Boundary Waters Canoe Area Wilderness.

Address/GPS for the Falls: Between Crocodile Lake and East Bearskin Lake; 48° 2'21.93" N, 90° 21'51.41" W.

Directions: If you've never visited here, it's best to hire a guide.

Website: None.

Waterway: Crocodile Creek.

Height: 12 feet. **Crest:** Varies.

Nearest Town: Grand Marais.

Hike Difficulty: Moderate. **Trail Quality:** Fair.

Round-trip Distance: 0.2 mile.

Admission: None.

Trip Report & Tips: I fully recommend staying a few nights at Bearskin Lodge, as this is the perfect way to fully enjoy the beauty around you. My girls and I canoed to Crocodile Falls on a drizzly, rainy, overcast June day with Quinn, our handy guide from Bearskin Lodge. We had just gotten an inch of rain over the previous 24 hours, so when we got to the falls, they were really flowing.

We paddled about 45 minutes on calm waters under heavily overcast skies heading over to the southern shore of East Bearskin Lake. There, you'll find a nice small area to leave behind your canoe and backpacks. After a short 0.1-mile hike full of wiggling your way around small pine trees and rocks, you'll find yourself in front of very impressive 12-foot falls. It flows over black rocks and surrounded by a dense wooded area of ash and cedar trees. After spending a few minutes there, we headed back on the narrow path full of new-growth evergreens to our waiting canoe.

Location: Boundary Waters Canoe Area Wilderness.

Address/GPS for the Falls: The southwest corner of Rose Lake at the Stairway Portage in the Boundary Waters Canoe Area Wilderness; near the Canadian border; 48° 5'32.81" N, 90° 26'39.33" W.

Directions: The southwest corner of Rose Lake at the Stairway Portage in the BWCAW. From Grand Marais, drive 28 miles up the Gunflint Trail. Turn right on Cty. Rd. 65 (also known as Hungry Jack Rd.) and drive 2 miles. You'll see the Hungry Jack Lodge entrance on your right. Head to the main lodge area for info and canoe rental.

Website: www.hungryjacklodge.com

Waterway: A creek that connects Duncan Lake to Rose Lake.

Height: 25 feet. **Crest:** 8 feet.

Nearest Town: Grand Marais.

Hike Difficulty: Good. **Trail Quality:** Good.

Round-trip Distance: A 6-mile paddle.

Admission: See page 7 for information about BWCAW permits.

Trip Report & Tips: We started at Hungry Jack Lodge, where we got tips from the helpful staff. On Hungry Jack Lake, we paddled east about 12 minutes to a secluded bay off to our left for the first short portage (to Bearskin Lake). The portage brings you across a parking lot and to the BWCAW permit box. From there, follow the trail and head down to Bearskin Lake. The paddle across Bearskin Lake is a quick and easy one. You'll first head north and then swerve to the left, paddling northwest; you'll easily see the portage to Duncan Lake as the land pinches together. This portage is about 0.2 mile. It starts off going uphill on a rocky trail, but it's not too difficult. Get your canoe back in the water and be careful around all the slippery rocks. On Duncan Lake, paddle approximately 25–40 minutes to the northeast end of the lake. There are many dead trees near the portage. After the portage, you can leave your canoe/gear and hike the 0.1 mile to Rose Lake and the falls. Veer right and let 30 wooden steps and the sound of the falls lead you to a great vantage point at the top of the falls.

Location: About 6 miles north of Ely on the Bass Lake Trail on the edge of the Boundary Waters Canoe Area Wilderness.

Address/GPS for the Falls: 47° 57'27.26" N, 91° 51'50.27" W.

Directions: Head east 1 mile out of Ely on U.S. Hwy. 169. Turn left on Cty. Rd. 88 and drive 2.2 miles, then turn right on Echo Trail and go 2.4 miles. You'll pass Echo Shores Resort on your left. The Bass Lake Trail parking lot will then be on your right. Park there. When you find the outhouse, you've found the beginning of the trail. Follow the signs; the trails are very well marked.

Website: www.ely.org/things-to-do/hiking

Waterway: An unnamed stream between Dry Lake flowing into Bass Lake.

Height: The Upper Falls are 8 feet; the Lower Falls are 6 feet. **Crest:** Varies.

Nearest Town: Ely.

Hike Difficulty: Moderate. **Trail Quality:** Fair.

Round-trip Distance: 1.8 miles.

Admission: None.

Trip Report & Tips: From the vault toilet, hike about 0.2 mile to where the trail splits. Take the Dry Falls route for 0.7 mile to the falls area. The trail is pretty rough, rocky and rugged, so wear sturdy shoes or boots. The trail rises 60 feet in elevation, so you'll be impressed by the beautiful vistas. At 0.7 mile, Bass Lake will appear on your right. As you are walking, notice the Ely Greenstone, an ancient metamorphic rock that formed several billion years ago. When the trail becomes rocky and starts really heading downward, you're getting close. At the falls area, you'll come to a very steep, rocky cliff. I suggest you walk all around first, as you can see the falls from all sides except the lakeside. As you head back, look for the wooden pedestrian bridge. From there you can see that the stream heads under the bridge; the river is then split by a large rock that forms two adjacent 8-foot waterfalls. One is wild and the other one has lacy fingers coming down to form what we called the "hot tub." This is an awesome area to rock climb, picnic, go swimming, or just sit and relax. In all, we spent an hour at the falls area.

Ash River Falls

Location: On the Ash River (access via boat).

Address/GPS for the Falls: 10418 Ash River Trail, Orr, 55771; 48° 22'38.55" N, 92° 49'11.27" W.

Directions: I'm going to use Ash Trail Lodge as my starting point since that's where my girls and I stayed and they took excellent care of us. You will find the falls just a bit over a mile south heading upstream from Ash Trail Lodge.

Website: www.ashtraillodge.com

Waterway: Ash River.

Height: The four-tiered waterfall tumbles a total of 34.5 feet.

Crest: Varies.

Nearest Town: Orr.

Hike Difficulty: Moderate if you get out of the boat, as there are huge rocks to tackle if you want to climb to the top of the steep falls.

Trail Quality: There is no trail; you'll be scrambling on rocks if you get out of the boat.

Round-trip Distance: Just over 2 river miles.

Admission: None.

Trip Report & Tips: Heading upstream, you will see the falls off to your left. They will be flowing over a huge gray rock face and coming down in four tiers. Try to scoot your boat, kayak or canoe over to the left side of the giant rock and hop out. If you explore the area up on top, you'll see multiple falls on both sides. While you are up at the top, you'll see that the river comes around the corner, sweeping past huge boulders, and drops down over four main levels. We visited in late July, and the falls were only 5–6 feet wide, but during May and early June, they can be as wide as the entire rock face. If you come when the river is really running, be careful when navigating your boat in the secluded bay, as you may get pushed back by the water's force.

Big Falls

Location: Big Falls Municipal Campground.

Address/GPS for the Falls: 123 Whispering Pine Dr., Big Falls, 56627; 48° 11'46.07" N, 93° 48'11.73" W.

Directions: Just north of Big Falls off Hwy. 71 on Whispering Pine Drive.

Website: www.bigfalls.govoffice.com

Waterway: Big Fork River.

Height: There are multiple falls and cascades; they range from 4–12 feet.

Crest: Varies.

Nearest Town: Big Falls.

Hike Difficulty: Easy. **Trail Quality:** Good.

Round-trip Distance: 0.2 mile.

Admission: It costs $25 a night to camp.

Trip Report & Tips: The Big Falls Municipal Campground is the access point for these falls. To reach it, drive down into the picnic area surrounded by tall white pines and find a parking spot by the restrooms. You can first head out to the large, rocky overlook to view the good-sized cascades that fall just after the Hwy. 71 bridge. Hike downriver about 0.1 mile to see the "real" Big Falls. Depending on the water level, you may need to do some rock hopping, and it's here that you will see that the river flows together like cars merging in traffic. The Big Falls flow down 8–12 feet on different levels. As you look around, you'll notice signs of high spring water levels, including huge logs pushed onto the rocks. When you look upstream, you'll see that the river has many miniature waterfalls, rapids and cascades and that they stretch all the way from the Hwy. 71 bridge downriver.

Upper Seagull Falls

Location: Trail's End Campground, at the end of the Gunflint Trail on the edge of the BWCAW.

Address/GPS for the Falls: 48° 9'16.92" N, 90°53'52.67" W.

Directions: Head to Trail's End Campground, which is 55 miles up the Gunflint Trail. Park by campsite 18, 19 or 20, but before you do, ask for permission first at the Trail's End Cafe. Campsite 20 is the closest to the Upper Falls.

Website: www.fs.usda.gov/recarea/superior/recreation/recarea/?recid=37013&actid=29

Waterway: Seagull River.

Height: 8–10 feet. **Crest:** 35 feet.

Nearest Town: Grand Marais.

Hike Difficulty: Moderate; there are some steep areas and big rocks. **Trail Quality:** Fair.

Round-trip Distance: 0.4 mile.

Admission: None.

Trip Report & Tips: There are two sections of Seagull Falls. The Upper Falls plunge about 8 feet, and on the way downstream they wind around rocks and trees, making for an impressive sight. You can reach the top of the falls via boulder climbing or take the trail downstream a bit to catch a distant view of the falls from a waterlogged tree situated partially in the river. When you go, be sure to bring bug spray and tick repellent and wear waterproof boots.

Lower Seagull Falls

Location: Trail's End Campground, at the end of the Gunflint Trail on the edge of the BWCAW.

Address/GPS for the Falls: 48° 9'19.79" N, 90° 53'53.48" W.

Directions: Head to Trail's End Campground, which is 55 miles up the Gunflint Trail. Park by campsite 18, 19 or 20, but before you do, ask for permission first at the Trail's End Cafe. Campsite 18 is the closest to the Lower Falls.

Website: www.fs.usda.gov/recarea/superior/recreation/recarea/?recid=37013&actid=29

Waterway: Seagull River.

Height: 8–10 feet. **Crest:** 35 feet.

Nearest Town: Grand Marais.

Hike Difficulty: Moderate; there are some steep areas and big rocks.

Trail Quality: Fair.

Round-trip Distance: 0.4 mile.

Admission: None.

Trip Report & Tips: You will find the lower set of cascading falls near campsite 18. Here the river comes around the corner and then plunges down. In all, there are 3 short drops for a total of about 8–10 feet. Seeing both the Upper and Lower Seagull Falls is a great way to start off (or end) a trip into the Boundary Waters.

Wolf Creek Falls

Banning State Park

An idyllic falls, Wolf Creek Falls
is situated among Banning State
Park's 6,255 acres.

Located at beautiful Banning State Park, Wolf Creek Falls is quite secluded, so much so that it's almost like having your own private waterfall!

Location: Banning State Park.

Address/GPS for the Falls: 61101 Banning Park Rd., Sandstone 55072; 46° 8'48.20" N, 92° 51'39.87" W.

Directions: Exit off of I-35 at Exit 195 (Banning Junction). Turn right, and the state park will be on your right.

Website: www.dnr.state.mn.us/state_parks/banning/index.html

Waterway: Wolf Creek.

Nearest Town: Sandstone.

Height: 12 feet. **Crest:** Varies.

Hike Difficulty: Easy.

Trail Quality: Good (but bring bug spray!).

Round-trip Distance: 1.4 miles.

Admission: A day pass at the state park is $5. A yearly vehicle pass is $25 and allows you to enter all state parks for a year.

Trip Report & Tips: The easiest way to access these falls is to camp at
the state park, as the trail to the falls begins at the campground. If you're
not camping at the park, ask for permission at the Visitor Center to park
at the campground (or just hike down Wolf Creek Trail from the Visitor
Center). Starting from the campground parking lot, it's a 1.4-mile round
trip and a relatively easy hike. We went on a dreary Mother's Day and
met no one on the trail. The minute after my daughter and I got into
the car from finishing our hike, it absolutely poured, so I guess we timed
it pretty well.

From the campground, hike 0.6 mile back to a very rocky area on the
Wolf Creek Trail. When you reach this massive rocky area, you'll know
that you are close to the falls. To get closer, you'll have to make your way
across the rocks because there really isn't a visible trail. You'll see the
Kettle River to your left and Wolf Creek will be on your right. When you
reach Wolf Creek Falls, plan on spending some time at this secluded area.
It may be only you and the mosquitoes. When we visited, my daughter
found some fallen trees to climb across and a sandy area to play and
keep her occupied. Because of its secluded nature, and the vivid colors
of the surrounding iron-rich rocks, this is truly one of Minnesota's more
unique falls. If you go during peak fall colors, you'll definitely be in for a
beautiful treat!

Tischer Creek Falls

Congdon Park

One of Duluth's true hidden gems, Tischer Creek Falls consists of multiple falls nestled in a rocky gorge. If you go in the spring, you'll be amazed at the water's power.

Tischer Creek Falls has it all: stunning falls, beautiful scenery and ease of access, as it's located in the heart of Duluth.

Location: Congdon Park.

Address/GPS for the Falls: On Superior St. between N 33rd Ave. E and Congdon Park Dr.; 46° 49'7.99" N, 92° 3'28.33" W.

Directions: Park near the intersection of E Superior and Congdon Park Dr.

Website: http://duluthtrails.com/congdon-park/

Waterway: Tischer Creek.

Nearest Town: Duluth.

Height: Varies by season. **Crest:** Varies.

Hike Difficulty: Easy. **Trail Quality:** Good.

Round-trip Distance: 0.6 mile.

Admission: None.

Trip Report & Tips: Start out by heading to the corner of Congdon Park; there you'll see the landscaped park sign. From the corner, head down 30 steps to the riverbank and hike across the first bridge. You'll notice it's slightly tilted and it looks kind of awkward; this is the first of three bridges you'll encounter. Nora and I journeyed through this awesome gorge on May 11th. It was 39 degrees and drizzling, and we were stunned by the volume of water raging through the deep canyon walls. It was *loud* down there. The hike is only 0.3 mile, but you'll see falls after falls after falls. It's incredible. We called our final falls 'The Grand Finale Falls," and when you see them you'll know why we named them that. The water tumbles down at three different levels between the red rock and crosses underneath a couple of downed trees. The red rock you'll see here is rhyolite, and formed over 1 billion years ago from lava. The park's namesake might also sound familiar: The 38-acre park was donated to the city by Chester A. Congdon in 1908. He and his wife, Clara, built the famous Glensheen Mansion. It is there that the Tischer Creek empties into Lake Superior.

When you visit, check out the nearby waterfalls on Chester Creek (pages 90-91), Amity Creek and Seven Bridges Rd. (pages 92-95) and the falls on the Lester River (pages 96-99).

Location: Jay Cooke State Park.

Address/GPS for the Falls: 80 Hwy. 210, Carlton, 55718; Swinging Bridge Falls: 46° 39'9.80" N, 92° 22'16.81" W; St. Louis Falls: 46° 39'11.85" N, 92° 22'19.72" W.

Directions: Located south of Duluth and Cloquet. Take Exit 235 off of I-35 and head east on Hwy. 210 for 3.8 miles to the park entrance. 1.5 miles into the park you'll find the visitor center on your right-hand side. Pull into that area and you'll find a spacious parking lot. If you park facing the river, the swinging bridge will be right in front of you.

Website: www.dnr.state.mn.us/state_parks/jay_cooke

Waterway: St. Louis River.

Height: These multi-tiered falls vary; usually from 5–14 feet. **Crest:** Varies.

Nearest Town: Carlton.

Hike Difficulty: Easy. **Trail Quality:** Good.

Round-trip Distance: 0.3 mile.

Admission: A day pass at the state park is $5. A yearly vehicle pass is $25 and allows you to enter all state parks for a year.

Trip Report & Tips: From the parking lot, head down toward the mighty St. Louis River. In the spring it is guaranteed to be running fast and fierce. In fact, on June 20, 2012, the water levels rose so high that it wiped out the suspension bridge and damaged much of the park. As you head out on the (repaired) bridge and face right, you'll see Swinging Bridge Falls off to your left and St. Louis Falls will be to the right. Keep hiking to the end of the bridge and take a right. You'll find yourself climbing up, over and around the black slate rocks to find your perfect viewing point.

The park is named for Jay Cooke, a Philadelphia banker who helped raise hundreds of millions of dollars for the Union war effort in the Civil War. After the war, he invested in the Northern Pacific Railway, and he soon visited Duluth, which he sought to transform into a second Chicago. Cooke died in 1905; his heirs donated the land for Jay Cooke State Park.

Location: Lincoln Park, Duluth.

Address/GPS for the Falls: At the intersection of 3rd St. and 25th Ave. W; First Falls: 46° 45'56.29" N, 92° 8'3.70.

Directions: From Chester Falls head down to Superior St. Keep going west on Superior St. to 25th Ave. W. Turn right on 25th Ave. W and go north to W 3rd St. Turn left on 3rd and the Lincoln Park entrance is on your right. You can also take the 27th Ave. exit off of I-35 (Exit 254).

Website: www.duluthmn.gov/parks/parks-listing/

Waterway: Miller Creek.

Height: There are four falls here, and while none are especially high, they are quite long. The first waterfall you see is 200 feet long (we measured!). **Crest:** 37 feet at the top.

Nearest Town: Duluth.

Hike Difficulty: Easy. **Trail Quality:** Good.

Round-trip Distance: 0.7 mile up to the third and fourth falls.

Admission: None.

Trip Report & Tips: When you pull into the park, the first falls will be on your left. This urban park will be busy if you visit on a summer weekend. As you head over to view the 200-foot-long waterfall, you'll see a short, manmade rock wall. After the first falls, you have the choice of hopping back in your car and driving to each of the falls, or taking your time and walking to each one. The second waterfall area my girls and I visited was just 0.3 mile up the park road. Once you're there, head to the pedestrian bridge, high over the creek, and look over either side into the deep gorge, which is about 8 feet wide. You'll find two additional picturesque falls located 0.7 mile from the park entrance at N 25th Ave. W and Lincoln Park Dr.; the creek will be on your right. Walk onto the bridge to view the 35-foot-wide cascades. There is a little waterfall pinched in the middle of all the rock. The other waterfall can be viewed by taking a right before the pedestrian bridge and heading down toward the creek. Miller Creek flows under the bridge, cascades down 5 feet and then plummets 13 feet on its way to Lake Superior.

Big Spring Falls

Location: Banning State Park.

Address/GPS for the Falls: 61101 Banning Park Rd., Sandstone 55072; 46° 6'48.15" N, 92° 51'29.05" W.

Directions: From Banning State Park, take a left and go west on Hwy. 23 to the T. Turn left and go south on Hwy. 23 to the city of Sandstone. (You will cross over I-35 twice.) Turn left on Hwy. 123, and go 0.3 mile and turn right on Pine Ave., right before you cross the Kettle River. When we were there, the road was not marked; look for it near the Lion's Hill sign. Go 0.2 mile on Pine Ave. and it will then turn to gravel. Go 0.7 mile farther down the bumpy gravel road. You'll see the trail map/trailhead on your left and there will be a place to park. If you go to the end of the road, you'll reach the Sandstone Rapids and the old hydroelectric dam on the Kettle River.

Website: www.dnr.state.mn.us/state_parks/banning/

Waterway: Kettle River.

Height: The three falls here vary from 5–10 feet.

Crest: The falls span the width of the river.

Nearest Town: Sandstone.

Hike Difficulty: Easy. **Trail Quality:** Good.

Round-trip Distance: 0.8 mile from parking lot down to the base of the falls and back.

Admission: A day pass at the state park is $5. A yearly vehicle pass is $25 and allows you to enter all state parks for a year.

Trip Report & Tips: There are three falls areas scattered around a huge table of exposed bedrock. The falls almost create a pinwheel going around the table rock. The falls area is easy to view from afar. After a quick 5-minute hike, you'll find the wide and crazy waterfall and its whitewater rapids. As you hike to the river bottom, you'll find a ladder situated near a large rock; this will take you down to the falls.

Kingsbury Creek Falls

Location: Lake Superior Zoo.

Address/GPS for the Falls: 7210 Fremont St, Duluth; 46° 43'36.48" N, 92° 11'34.29" W.

Directions: Located in south Duluth.

Website: www.lszooduluth.org

Waterway: Kingsbury Creek.

Height: Falls drop around 60 feet under 2 bridges.

Crest: Varies.

Nearest Town: Duluth.

Hike Difficulty: Easy. **Trail Quality:** Good.

Round-trip Distance: 0.6 mile.

Admission: Adults, $10; Children, $5 (2 and under are free).

Trip Report & Tips: Located on the campus of the Lake Superior Zoo. Start out by paying admission in the gift shop, then head downstairs and out the back door to view the outdoor zoo animals. You'll find the falls if you head out to the right, passing by the eagle enclosure. If you go in springtime, just listen for the falls and you'll find them. The falls are pretty from a distance, and more dramatic if you go up closer to the bridge.

Once you've seen the falls, check out the rest of the zoo. It has a nice variety of animals, including lions, a bear, a snow leopard, wolves, a tiger, a lynx, lemurs, a bald eagle, as well as barnyard animals. You may also see peacocks and geese roaming around the grounds.

Oldenburg Cascades

Location: Jay Cooke State Park.

Address/GPS for the Falls: 780 Hwy. 210, Carlton, 55718; 46° 39'5.00" N, 92° 21'9.58" W.

Directions: Located south of Cloquet. On I-35 take Exit 235 to Carlton. Drive 3.8 miles east on Hwy. 210 to the Jay Cook State Park entrance. From the entrance sign, it's 2.6 miles to Oldenburg Point Picnic areas; the parking lot will be on your right.

Website: www.dnr.state.mn.us/state_parks/jay_cooke/index.html

Waterway: St. Louis River.

Height: Varies by season. **Crest:** Varies.

Nearest Town: Carlton.

Hike Difficulty: Easy to the overlook; strenuous heading down to the river.

Trail Quality: Good to the overlook; very poor heading down to the river.

Round-trip Distance: 0.2 mile to the overlook; 0.6 mile to the cascades.

Admission: A day pass at the state park is $5. A yearly vehicle pass is $25 and allows you to enter all state parks for a year.

Trip Report & Tips: From the parking lot, pass the picnic shelter and head 0.1 mile to the Oldenburg Point overlook. Here you will see panoramic views of the St. Louis River Valley. If you're looking for more adventure, head down to river level. As you walk by the overlook, you'll see a heavily worn path to the right at the edge of the low rock wall. Take the path and follow the narrow trail down a steep hill to 55 slate steps. From here it is 0.2 mile down to the river. After the uneven slate steps it becomes a very steep path down to the river's edge. Use extreme caution if going down to the river.

Blue Nude Falls

Location: Duluth.

Address/GPS for the Falls: 46° 45'1.37" N, 92° 11'8.74" W.

Directions: From I-35 take the Skyline Pkwy. exit and drive 2.3 miles to the stop sign. Take a right on Vinland St. and head to the stop sign. Cross over Highland St. and take an immediate right into the paved parking lot for the Highland/Gretchell trailhead of the Superior Hiking Trail.

Website: None.

Waterway: Keene Creek.

Height: The main falls are 10 feet high. **Crest:** Varies.

Nearest Town: Duluth.

Hike Difficulty: Moderate to strenuous heading down to the creek.

Trail Quality: Poor.

Round-trip Distance: 0.2 mile.

Admission: None.

About Keene Creek: Keene Creek feeds into the St. Louis River.

Trip Report & Tips: From the parking lot, head down toward the creek and the old bridge, which isn't very far from the parking lot. Take some time to explore all around. When you get to the bridge, turn right and head down to view all the cool graffiti underneath the bridge. If you're lucky, you'll be able to see the painting of the blue nude. She's getting pretty weathered, so you may have to look hard; she's at the top of the falls. Here the creek begins to fall 10 feet as it winds its way downward over a four-level cascade. It's then followed by three more mini waterfalls. The creek splits and then reunites; to view this area, you'll want to hike downstream a bit holding onto some trees for help over to the creek. Note: You may want to put on your tall waterproof boots for this hidden gem.

Chester Bowl Falls

Location: Chester Bowl Park.

Address/GPS for the Falls: 1801 E Skyline Pkwy., Duluth, 55812; 46° 48'45.85" N, 92° 5'24.95" W.

Directions: From Superior St., drive north up 15th Ave. E. It turns into Chester Park Dr. Take it all the way up (passing the pretty houses) to Chester Bowl park's parking lot. Note: Right before the parking lot, Chester Park Dr. turns into Skyline Pkwy.

Website: www.chesterbowl.org

Waterway: Chester Creek.

Height: 40-plus feet of cascades and waterfalls.

Crest: Varies.

Nearest Town: Duluth.

Hike Difficulty: Moderate; fairly steep.

Trail Quality: Good.

Round-trip Distance: 0.3 mile.

Admission: None.

Trip Report & Tips: Along with Lincoln and Zenith parks, Chester Park is one of Duluth's original three parks. To get to the falls, head down to Chester Creek on a few stone steps and under the bridge on the sidewalk. Then you can head down the path or follow the river cascading down the hill. The river is chiseled down through the rocks. The Main Falls area is around 40 feet long and made up of multiple falls. The waterfalls really start after the river goes under the bridge and fall among the rocks until the river levels out. Keep in mind that on the weekends this is a busy area, with lots of kids climbing around on the rocks. It is definitely worth a visit, though, as it's unique to visit a big-city park and suddenly feel like you're no longer in the city.

Big Ten Falls

Location: Chester Bowl Park

Address/GPS for the Falls: Along the Chester Creek Trail; 46° 48'32.79" N, 92° 5'20.15" W.

Directions: From E Superior St., drive north up 15th Ave. E., which turns into Chester Park Dr. Take that all the way to N 17th Ave. E, then park on the side of the road.

Website: None.

Waterway: Chester Creek.

Height: 10 feet.   **Crest:** 7 feet.

Nearest Town: Duluth.

Hike Difficulty: Moderate to strenuous; it's steep going down but a bit easier coming up.

Trail Quality: Good if you view from above; poor if you head down to river level.

Round-trip Distance: 0.2 mile.

Admission: None.

Trip Report & Tips: If you parked on the corner of N 17th Ave. E and Chester Park Drive, head across the road and look for the path and steps just before 17th Ave. Here you will find 78 steps that lead you right to the footbridge on top of the falls. Cross the bridge and turn left. You will find a steep trail heading down to the river's edge. It is a strenuous hike to get down to the river level, so you'll likely need to grab onto some tree branches for assistance on the steep decline. A visit to the falls is worth it, as not only are there four mini waterfalls present, but the creek slopes down to meet a good-sized swimming hole. We visited the falls on July 23rd when the water levels were lower, and I could hardly get my girls to leave.

4th Street Bridge Falls

Location: Along the Chester Creek Trail.

Address/GPS for the Falls: 4th St. bridge and 14th Ave. E; 46° 48'10.49" N, 92° 5'8.63" W.

Directions: From Chester Bowl Park, head back down Chester Park Dr., which turns into 15th Ave. E. Turn right on 4th St. and park near the bridge right after you cross 14th Ave. E. You can stand on the bridge and view the waterfalls.

Website: None.

Waterway: Chester Creek.

Height: The upper falls are 8–10 feet; the two lower falls are approximately 15 feet.

Crest: Varies.

Nearest Town: Duluth.

Hike Difficulty: Very easy.

Trail Quality: View from bridge.

Round-trip Distance: Less than 0.1 mile.

Admission: None.

Trip Report & Tips: From your wonderful bridge vantage point you can clearly see the top waterfall flowing down into a small pool and then two more skinny waterfalls flowing down and hugging a massive rock formation in the middle. These falls land in a shallow pool down below.

Amity Creek Falls

Location: Lester Park.

Address/GPS for the Falls: Near the 500 block of Occidental Blvd.; 46° 50'37.55" N, 92° 0'34.95" W.

Directions: From Hwy. 61 (London Rd.) turn left onto 60th Ave. E. Then go 2 blocks and turn right on Superior St. Then turn left on Occidental Blvd, and go 0.3 mile; you'll see the park on the side of the road. Park around the 500 block of Occidental Blvd.; there, on the right-hand side, you'll see a wooden pedestrian bridge. (If you drive over an actual bridge on Occidental, you've gone too far, though there is a small gravel parking area after it.)

Website: www.duluthmn.gov/parks/

Waterway: Amity Creek.

Height: Depends on the water level; there are cascades down in two different areas.

Crest: Varies.

Nearest Town: Duluth.

Hike Difficulty: Easy. **Trail Quality:** Good.

Round-trip Distance: 0.1 mile.

Admission: None.

Trip Report & Tips: These falls are best viewed during high water levels. You can photograph them from the pedestrian bridge that goes over "The Deeps" waterfall on Amity Creek. You'll see the falls flowing downstream from the first bridge on Seven Bridges Rd. You can also get a closer look by hiking upstream on the east side of the creek. As the name suggests, the creek runs under seven historic bridges; they are made out of basalt and bluestone.

Amity Falls at "The Deeps"

Location: Lester Park.

Address/GPS for the Falls: Near the 500 block of Occidental Blvd.; 46° 50'37.16" N, 92° 0'34.37" W.

Directions: From Hwy. 61 (London Rd.) turn left onto 60th Ave. E. Then go 2 blocks and turn right on Superior St. and turn left on Occidental Blvd. and go 0.3 mile; you'll see the park on the side of the road. You can park on the side of the road by the gazebo that's on your right. (If you drive over an actual bridge on Occidental, you've gone too far.)

Website: None.

Waterway: Amity Creek.

Height: From the top it slopes down 44 feet.

Crest: 24 feet.

Nearest Town: Duluth.

Hike Difficulty: Easy. **Trail Quality:** Good.

Round-trip Distance: 0.2 mile

Admission: None.

Trip Report & Tips: Located in a nice neighborhood of Duluth and easy to find, this is a popular Duluth waterfall. If you parked near the gazebo, head down the steep rocky area down to the creek level. There are lots of rapids, waterfalls and swimming holes along Amity Creek. While most of Amity creek is shallow, there are some areas in The Deeps that reach 40 feet down, perfect for cliff jumpers; though be wary of actually cliff jumping here (or high water levels) because many injuries and even some deaths have occurred on site. If you are a more cautious type like me, there's plenty of fun to be had. Just put your rain boots on and hike along in the creek looking at cool rocks or hunt for little crabs. If you visit in the spring, the water levels will be high, so bring along a towel, as you will get sprayed.

Keep Smiling Falls

Location: Lester Park.

Address/GPS for the Falls: 46° 51'38.40" N, 92° 0'52.21" W.

Directions: From Hwy. 61 (London Rd.), turn left on 60th Ave. E. Go 2 blocks and turn right on Superior St. and just before you cross the bridge, turn left on Occidental Blvd., also known as Seven Bridges Rd.

Drive 1.3 miles from the first bridge until you reach the seventh and final bridge. You can either cross over the seventh bridge and park immediately on your right, or you can park in a small dirt pull-off area just before you cross the bridge. Keep Smiling Falls flows right under the seventh bridge.

Website: None.

Waterway: Amity Creek.

Height: 12 feet. **Crest:** Varies.

Nearest Town: Duluth.

Hike Difficulty: Easy. **Trail Quality:** Good.

Round-trip Distance: 0.1 mile.

Admission: None.

Trip Report & Tips: You can park on either side of the bridge and find good views. You can follow the trail down on the east side for a more secluded view; on the west side, by the dirt parking area, you can just head out on the rocks for a great viewing area. My first time seeing the falls was on a rainy May afternoon. The water was flowing quickly, and on some of my slower shutter speed images you could even see the rain drops coming down. If you want an especially pretty picture, stand out on the rocks with the water flowing right at you and the beautiful rock bridge will be in the background.

Japp Hole Waterfall

Location: Lester Park.

Address/GPS for the Falls: 61st Ave. E & Superior St; 46° 5 0'20.11" N, 92° 0'24.68" W.

Directions: From Hwy. 61 (London Rd) take a left onto 60th Ave. E. Follow this for two blocks, crossing the railroad tracks, and turn right on Superior St. Cross the Superior St. bridge and turn left on Lester River Rd. The parking lot for Lester Park will be on your left.

Website: www.duluthmn.gov/parks/

Waterway: Lester River.

Height: Tumbles down several different levels for a total height of 20–25 feet.

Crest: Varies.

Nearest Town: Duluth.

Hike Difficulty: Easy from the bridge; moderate if you head down for a closer look.

Trail Quality: Fair.

Round-trip Distance: 0.2 mile.

Admission: None.

Trip Report & Tips: From the Lester Park parking lot, walk back over to Superior St., cross the road and head for the railroad tracks, where you'll see a big, brown pedestrian bridge. Japp Hole Waterfall flows under the Superior St. bridge, hugging the right side of the river bank and flowing into Japp Hole. The pool is deep, and when water levels are high, the current can be intense. If you are visiting during lower water levels, you can get a closer look by walking across the Superior St. bridge and heading down to the river at the end of the bridge (on the Lester Park side). If you do, it will be a bit steep in areas, but you should be able to find a path and head down. My friends and I explored in late July when water levels were somewhat low and we could hop across rocks and walk under the bridge over to Japp Hole.

Gunderson's Waterfall

Location: Lester Park.

Address/GPS for the Falls: 61st Ave. E & Superior St.; 46° 50'23.39" N, 92° 0'23.76" W.

Directions: From Hwy. 61 (London Rd) take a left onto 60th Ave. E. Follow this for two blocks, crossing the railroad tracks, and turn right on Superior St. Cross the Superior St. bridge and turn left on Lester River Rd. The parking lot for Lester Park will be on your left.

Website: www.duluthmn.gov/parks/

Waterway: Lester River.

Height: 3 feet. **Crest:** 64 feet.

Nearest Town: Duluth.

Hike Difficulty: Easy. **Trail Quality:** Good.

Round-trip Distance: < 0.1 mile.

Admission: None.

Trip Report & Tips: From the Lester Park parking lot, head over the stone pedestrian bridge. Turn left and walk down the gravel path that is in between the Lester River and Amity Creek. You'll be walking toward a flag pole, and once you pass it, turn left again and go down 18 steep (and pretty unsafe!) stone steps. The last couple are very high up from the ground, so you'll need to assist kids here. If the river isn't flowing too fast, you can go down and swim in this area, climb around the cement ledge that forms Gunderson's Waterfall or just hang out in the sandy shore area. (You can also view Gunderson's from the Superior St. bridge or the west side of the river.) A number of other waterfalls are nearby; Japp Hole Falls, Lester Park Falls, The Deeps and Amity Creek Falls are all within a half-mile hike.

The Shallows

Location: Lester Park, Duluth.

Address/GPS for the Falls: 46° 50'39.75" N, 92° 0'13.36" W.

Directions: Heading northeast on Hwy. 61 (London Rd.), take a left onto 60th Ave. E, then go two blocks, cross the railroad tracks and turn right on Superior St. Then cross the Superior St. bridge and turn left on Lester River Rd. Drive 0.3 mile on Lester River Rd. and park on the left side of the road. (If you drive past the Lester Park Golf Course, you've gone too far.) Once you've parked, look for the gravel path leading down to the river.

Website: www.duluthmn.gov/parks/

Waterway: Lester River.

Height: Slopes down 45 feet. **Crest:** 21 feet.

Nearest Town: Duluth.

Hike Difficulty: Moderate.

Trail Quality: Fair to poor.

Round-trip Distance: 0.2 mile.

Admission: None.

Trip Report & Tips: As you head down the gravel trail, you'll come to 28 stone steps that will lead you down to the Lester River. Once you are down there, walk along the riverside and make your way back to the falls. Be careful: It is kind of tricky to maneuver among the rocks along the river. At 45 feet, The Shallows is the tallest of all the Lester River falls and it slopes down over a jagged wall of rocks before entering the river.

Lower Gooseberry Falls

One of the must-sees of the
North Shore, Gooseberry Falls
is incredibly popular.

I enjoy visiting Gooseberry in the morning before most tourists get up. Better yet, the early morning light is perfect for photography.

Location: Gooseberry Falls State Park.

Address/GPS for Falls: 3206 Highway 61 E Two Harbors, 55616; 47° 8'33.70"N, 91° 28'1.83"W.

Directions: 12 miles NE of Two Harbors or 5 miles SW of Split Rock Light House at mile marker 39 on Hwy 61.

Website: www.dnr.state.mn.us/state_parks/gooseberry_falls

Waterway: Gooseberry River.

Nearest Town: Two Harbors.

Height: The Lower Falls are 40 feet high.

Crest: Varies.

Hike Difficulty: Easy. **Trail Quality:** Good, mostly paved, with some boardwalk and a few steps.

Round-trip Distance: 1 mile for the Lower and Middle Falls, although it really depends on how much hiking you do around the falls.

Admission: None. Even though the waterfalls are located on the grounds of the state park, a state park sticker is not needed to view the falls.

Trip Report & Tips: Gooseberry State Park is one of the more popular state parks in Minnesota, welcoming around half a million visitors annually. It's easy to understand why: The sightseeing is amazing, the waterfalls are beautiful (especially when the water levels are up), the trails are mostly paved and it's a short distance to four waterfalls. The falls, which are simply named the Upper, Middle and Lower Falls (of which there are two), plummet down a combined 95 feet on their way to Lake Superior.

They are also a lot of fun to photograph during any season. To find the falls, just head past the visitor center and follow the signs. The Falls Loop Trail goes all the way around both sides of the Middle and Lower Falls, and it also lets you see them from different levels. On the west side of the river is a boardwalk and steps bringing you downstream to a footbridge. This is one of my favorite areas to photograph the Lower and Middle Falls together. Head across the bridge over to the east side of the river for a more rugged trail and great higher elevation views. As the Middle Falls flow down over a very long rocky ledge, look for the large "rock island" in the river before the water plummets down to the Lower Falls, where the Gooseberry River splits in two, to form the bottom beauties.

If you like to hike, the park has 18 miles of picturesque trails. Or head up to Fifth Falls (page 190), which is a 2.2-mile round-trip hike from the visitor center. Inside the visitor center you'll find information about Lake Superior, agates, wolves and the history of Gooseberry Falls and the region. The park also boasts one of the biggest and best gift shops on the North Shore. If you want anything "Minnesota," this is the place to find it.

High Falls on the Baptism River

If you want tall waterfalls, then this is the place for you. Other than the High Falls of Pigeon River, which Minnesota shares with Canada, the High Falls on the Baptism River is the tallest waterfall in the state.

An amazing park that's fabulous in all seasons, Tettegouche is home to the High Falls, the tallest waterfall that is entirely located in Minnesota.

Location: Tettegouche State Park.

Address/GPS for the Falls: 5702 Hwy. 61, Silver Bay, 55614; 47° 21'4.32" N, 91° 12'35.77" W.

Directions: Located 4.5 miles northeast of Silver Bay on Hwy. 61 near mile marker 59.

Website: www.dnr.state.mn.us/state_parks/tettegouche/index.html

Waterway: Baptism River.

Nearest Town: Silver Bay.

Height: The High Falls are 60 feet. **Crest:** Varies.

Hike Difficulty: Moderate to strenuous.

Trail Quality: Good.

Round-trip Distance: 2 to 3 miles, depending on your choice of trail.

Admission: A day pass at the state park is $5. A yearly vehicle pass is $25 and allows you to enter all state parks for a year.

Trip Report & Tips: High Falls is the tallest waterfall located entirely within Minnesota; at 60 feet high, it's a sight to behold, especially when the river water level is up. To reach the falls, you have three options. You can drive over to the main campground and park in its lot, then head over on either the Superior Hiking Trail or walk through the campground and take a shortcut trail back to the falls. The third option is to drive down from the visitor center and toward the river, where you can park in the fisherman's parking lot and hike 1.5 miles (one way) to the High Falls.

Whichever option you choose, be aware that a hike down to the Baptism River is not an easy one. It involves climbing up/down many steps, and this can be tiring. My friend Sue and I took the Superior Hiking Trail on the way into the falls and the shorter campground trail on our return hike back to the parking lot. If you take the Superior Trail, after ascending many steps, you'll eventually reach a viewing platform on top of the falls, and then a suspension bridge. If you cross over the bridge, you'll head to a wide-open area with a great view of the falls.

If you prefer the third option, the fisherman's parking lot is located right before the bridge that crosses over the river. There, you'll see a sign on the right that indicates it's 1 mile to Two-Step Falls and 1.5 miles to High Falls.

The Cascades on the Baptism River

Something of a hidden gem, the Cascades on the Baptism River are truly an awe-inspiring sight, especially when the river is really running fast.

Getting to the Cascades on the Baptism River involves quite a few steps, but don't let that dissuade you. The hike is surprisingly fast, and fun!

Location: Tettegouche State Park.

Address/GPS for the Falls: 5702 Hwy. 61, Silver Bay, 55614; 47° 20'31.94" N, 91° 12'24.24" W.

Directions: Located 4.5 miles northeast of Silver Bay on Hwy. 61 near mile marker 59.

Website: www.dnr.state.mn.us/state_parks/tettegouche/

Waterway: Baptism River.

Nearest Town: Silver Bay.

Height: 20–25 feet. **Crest:** Varies.

Hike Difficulty: Easy; you'll need to navigate 248 steps on your one-way hike, but they are spread out enough that it's not much of a burden. When I hiked with a pal, it only took 25 minutes to get back to the truck from the falls area.

Trail Quality: Good.

Round-trip Distance: 2 miles.

Admission: A day pass at the state park is $5. A yearly vehicle pass is $25 and allows you to enter all state parks for a year.

Trip Report & Tips: Park in the lot that is just southwest from the visitor center and situated just before the big bridge on the park road. Hike over the bridge crossing the Baptism River. You'll come to a brown sign that says "Cascades .75 miles dead ends." The trail then heads down a few steps and across a boardwalk to a nice packed trail up along the riverside. At 0.2 mile into your hike, you'll come to a bench and steps down to the river's edge. Take the 19 steps and continue along the trail, which is surrounded by birch and pines. At 0.4 mile you'll come down seven wooden steps. Head out over the river to view a 5-foot-high cascade. The trail then turns left and goes uphill. At 0.6 mile you'll cross a wooden footbridge. Listen to the relaxing river as you pass through a ferny area that may remind you of *Jurassic Park*. You'll then come to 23 wooden steps and the trail gets more adventurous. You'll take 14 steps down, 6 more steps down, cross a footbridge and then head up 45 steps. Next, you will be gliding down 21 steps, cross another footbridge and take 14 more wooden steps down. It sounds tiring, but it's not. Now the path narrows up right alongside the river. At 0.8 mile you'll take 19 steps down to reach the river bank. By now, you'll hear the Cascades ahead. Once you scoot around the corner, it's an awe-inspiring sight. The Cascades are majestic, yet secluded, and they're often yours to enjoy at your leisure since not as many people visit them (compared to, say, the High Falls). As you face the falls, the left side kicks around a 90-degree bend and falls down 20–25 feet. The right side wisps down a 45-degree rock slide with root beer-colored water and gets wider as it reaches the bottom. The Cascades are separated by a massive basalt boulder. If you enjoy scrambling on rocks, this is the place for you. Please use caution, as the rocks up and around the falls area are high up and you may need a helping hand from a friend. Still, it's definitely worth the effort to head up on top of the Cascades, as the view is incomparable. Enjoy these falls, as they're some of my favorites.

Caribou Falls, Caribou River

To reach these impressive 40-foot
falls, you'll need to hoof it down
quite a few stairs, but the falls
are lovely and situated quite close
to the Superior Hiking Trail,
giving you many other hiking
and exploring options.

With its relaxing hike that leads to a striking waterfall surrounded by otherworldly vegetation, Caribou Falls has a lot to offer. The only downside? Lots of steps to descend (and then climb back up).

Location: About 5 miles north of Little Marais.

Address/GPS for the Falls: 47° 28'7.84" N, 91° 1'54.50" W.

Directions: Park at the Caribou Falls Wayside Rest located at mile marker 70 on Hwy. 61 The wayside rest is very close to the county line dividing Cook and Lake Counties and quite close to the Superior Hiking Trail.

Website: http://dnr.state.mn.us/state_parks/waysides/index.html

Waterway: Caribou River.

Nearest Town: Little Marais.

Height: 35–40 feet. **Crest:** Varies.

Hike Difficulty: Moderate. **Trail Quality:** Fair.

Round-trip Distance: 1 mile for Caribou Falls; 1.5 miles to see a few more falls.

Admission: None.

Trip Report & Tips: Beginning from the Caribou Falls Wayside Rest, this hike starts as a nice leisurely stroll alongside the river. My friend Sue and I hiked this gem on a foggy and damp day in mid-May. As you pass by young evergreens, the path rises and you are able to view the birch-filled river valley. Even though the hike becomes a bit more difficult as you proceed, it is still very peaceful and beautiful. At a half mile in you will see (and hear) the loud, raging waterfall. You'll also see the 155 steps down to the river. Don't let this deter you, as you can worry about climbing back up later. (At least that's what I told myself.) When I got to the bottom of the steps, the water was washing over the lowest cement slab. At the top of Caribou Falls, the river plummets a bit and takes a little turn to drop down about 35 feet. The warped and wild trees are one of the most interesting characteristics about Caribou Falls; they grow at odd angles, seemingly straight out of the rock. This definitely makes a visit (and pictures) even more alluring. After you're satisfied with the main Caribou Falls, you'll need to climb up the steps and then decide if you want to visit more falls or just head back to the car. Sue and I chose to travel on. If you have the energy, hiking a little bit farther up along the Caribou River is definitely worth it, though I have to admit that I found myself wishing for a Caribou Coffee somewhere on this trail.

Keep hiking upward and be careful, as you will be up very high. There is even a sign posted warning you to keep children at hand. After 0.4 mile, you will come to a very large wooden viewing platform and a bridge that crosses the river. When Sue and I reached this area we both had a feeling that we were being watched. I watched and waited for a bear to pop out of the woods, though we didn't see one. Still, after this trip I brought a whistle along just in case of emergencies. (I haven't used it yet, thank goodness.) Bears or not (hopefully not!), enjoy all the beautiful falls and cascades along the Caribou River and have a safe hike!

The Cascades on the Manitou River

Prepare yourself for a moderate
hike through the dense woods.
You'll be fully rewarded by these
magnificent falls. Go in the fall
for beautiful color.

A mighty falls amid the backcountry of George H. Crosby Manitou State Park, the Cascades consist of three tiers that fall around 50 feet over the course of 200 feet.

Location: George H. Crosby Manitou State Park.

Address/GPS for the Falls: 7616 Lake Cty. Rd. 7; 47° 29'14.16" N, 91° 6'24.37" W.

Directions: At mile marker 59 on Hwy. 61, turn north on Hwy. 1 and travel 6.1 miles to the little village of Finland. After you cross over the Baptism River, turn right on Cty. Rd. 7 and drive 7.5 miles. You will be on blacktop the first 1.2 miles and the rest is a well-maintained gravel road. Look for the Crosby Manitou State Park sign and turn into the park.

Website: www.dnr.state.mn.us/state_parks/george_crosby_manitou

Waterway: Manitou River.

Nearest Town: Finland.

Height: 50 feet. **Crest:** The Cascades are as wide as the river, which varies significantly.

Hike Difficulty: Moderate on the way back to the Cascades and moderately strenuous on the hike back to the parking lot. **Trail Quality:** Fair to poor.

Round-trip Distance: 2 miles.

Admission: A day pass at the state park is $5. A yearly vehicle pass is $25 and allows you to enter all state parks for a year.

Trip Report & Tips: Once you enter the park, go a half mile back to a large parking lot. You are going to want the middle trail; it's the one closest to the vault toilet. At 0.3 mile into your hike, you'll come to a nice boardwalk area going across a little stream. Twenty minutes along on your hike or about 0.6 mile, there will be a campsite. A little bit farther down the trail you'll come to a fork in the path. Go left on the Manitou River Trail and head down the 59 steps to the river's edge. When I ventured to the falls in mid-June, the falls were absolutely massive and mighty, and when I went back to see them in September, they were still flowing really well.

The Cascades are made up of three separate tiers that drop about 40–50 feet over a span of about 200 feet of water. While I was exploring the Cascades and photographing the falls, a young couple came over for their morning bath. All the backpack campsites are very primitive, and there are no showers anywhere nearby, so the Manitou River makes a nice, clean, chilly bathtub.

On the return hike, the first 0.2 mile will take you on a strenuous uphill climb. Just know that there is a bench waiting for you at the top of the hill where the Middle Trail splits with the River Trail. Take the Middle Trail back to the parking lot. Your return hike to the parking lot should take about 30 minutes. If you choose to head downstream from the Cascades to view the other falls, stay on the Manitou River Trail and do not take the Middle Trail back. Please note that this is a tiring and strenuous hike. Make sure you have plenty of water, bug spray and some snacks.

Onion River Falls

After a steep slide down to the riverside, you can get up close and personal with the Onion River Falls. If the water levels are right, the expansive bedrock nearby is the perfect place for a picnic.

Also known as "Stairstep Falls," the Onion River Falls tumble down several steps, giving the falls an elegant, almost lacy look.

Location: Ray Berglund Wayside Rest.

Address/GPS for the Falls: 47° 36'43.40" N, 90° 46'27.94" W.

Directions: At mile marker 86 on Hwy. 61; park at the Ray Berglund Wayside Rest.

Website: http://dnr.state.mn.us/state_parks/waysides/index.html

Waterway: Onion River.

Nearest Town: Tofte.

Height: 42 feet. **Crest:** 18–24 feet.

Hike Difficulty: Moderate. **Trail Quality:** Good.

Round-trip Distance: 0.8 mile

Admission: None.

Trip Report & Tips: Start out from the parking lot at the Ray Berglund Wayside Rest, then get ready to climb some stairs. In all, you'll need to surmount 53 wooden steps. At the top of the steps, follow the well-worn path to the left toward the river. At 0.2 mile in, you will come to the first overlook with both falls below you. There are no guardrails here, so be careful. After looking around, keep heading up the trail, which is surrounded by birch and pine. At 0.4 mile, take a left and head down to the river. Either slide on your bottom or carefully walk down; you'll probably need to hang onto trees and roots along the way, as this is a very steep area.

When we reached the river, my friend Sue and I took portraits of each other with the falls in the background. After the steep slide down, it's a fun area to just sit, relax and take it all in. There are lots of flat rocks down by the falls, so you may even want to have a little picnic while you're down there.

The Onion River takes three big steps down over black volcanic rock. For this reason it's sometimes called "Stair Step Falls." The first drop has two tiers and heads down about 32 feet. Here the water lingers in a relaxing pool. It then heads down another 10 feet as the river heads off to Lake Superior. When you're ready to hike back, take your time and be very careful climbing up the steep bank. It took us 10 minutes to get back to the parking lot from the riverside.

We photographed Onion Falls on May 19th, but if you venture here in late summer or fall, you should be able to walk along the riverbed on your way back to the falls, assuming the water levels are right.

Cascade Falls on the Cascade River

The Cascade River is home to
wild falls and crazy cascades
—and it's paralleled by the
Superior Hiking Trail, a trio
of wonderful ways to enjoy the
outdoors in Minnesota.

The Cascade River lives up to its name, as its root beer-colored water crashes dramatically over basalt ledges; it's also home to Cascade Falls, a 25-foot waterfall!

Location: Cascade Wayside Park.

Address/GPS for the Falls: 3481 W Hwy. 61, Lutsen, 55612; 47° 42'30.10" N, 90° 31'25.92" W.

Directions: Located at mile marker 100 on Hwy. 61. The park is 10 miles north of Lutsen Mountain and 9 miles south of Grand Marais.

Website: www.dnr.state.mn.us/state_parks/cascade_river

Waterway: Cascade River.

Nearest Town: Lutsen.

Height: 25–30 feet. **Crest:** Varies.

Hike Difficulty: Easy. **Trail Quality:** Good.

Round-trip Distance: 0.2 mile.

Admission: Parking at the wayside is free, but if you enter the adjacent state park, you'll need to purchase a $5 day pass. A yearly vehicle pass is $25 and allows you to enter all state parks for a year.

Trip Report & Tips: There is ample parking right at mile marker 100 near the Cascade River and just north of Cascade Lodge. Once you're parked, look for the sign that says "Cascade Falls 300 feet" and head up a few rock steps on the well-worn path that will lead you right to Cascade Falls, arguably the most popular falls on the North Shore.

On its final 13 miles before entering Lake Superior, the beautiful Cascade River drops over 900 feet over multiple falls, cascades and black lava rock ledges. The gorge the river runs through is filled with moss, ferns, white cedar, spruce and birch trees, and there is some excellent hiking nearby, as the Superior Hiking Trail runs parallel with the river on both sides. Cascade River State Park also boasts 18 miles of beautiful hiking trails.

Also, if you're looking for a place to stay in the area, Cascade Lodge is right next door. My friend Sue and I stayed in one of their two-bedroom motel units in the fall and it was great. We could hike right over to Cascade River State Park and cross Hwy. 61 to go sit by Lake Superior.

Thompson Falls, Cascade River

A little-known gem, Thompson Falls is well worth a visit, as it's one of the taller waterfalls in the state and far less frequented than more famous falls.

These falls are a great place to get away from it all, and they're only 20 miles from Lutsen and Hwy. 61.

Location: Just off the North Shore, located south of The Grade.

Address/GPS for the Falls: 47° 51'25.66" N, 90° 32'50.43" W.

Directions: From Lutsen, head north on the Caribou Trail (Cty. Rd. 4) and go all the way to the end of the trail, about 17.3 miles, until it meets "The Grade." The Grade is also known as Forest Rd. 153. Turn right on The Grade and drive east 2.4 miles to Forest Rd. 158 (Bally Creek Rd.). Turn right and head south on Forest Rd. 158 for only 0.2 mile. Look closely, and you'll see a small wooden sign marking Thompson Falls on your right, and there will be a small parking spot.

Website: None.

Waterway: Cascade River.

Nearest Town: Lutsen.

Height: 30–35 feet. **Crest:** Varies.

Hike Difficulty: Easy. **Trail Quality:** Fair.

Round-trip Distance: 0.2 mile.

Admission: None.

Trip Report & Tips: Once you are parked, head off to the trail on your right. It's a well-worn rocky path that will lead you past a section of the Cascade River that looks like a large marshy area. Keep hiking onward and the sound of crashing water will get louder. Find your way down to the base of the falls and have fun exploring this secluded area. When my friend Sue and I explored the area it was mid-May and the water was flowing with a vengeance over the sloped black rocks; huge white currents spilled over the falls, then fanned out wider as they hit the bottom. After the falls area, the Cascade River turns for a short spell and then splits in half among some trees.

When you visit, there's a good chance you'll have the place to yourself, as Thompson Falls is not especially well-known. In fact, I'd only heard of the falls once, having read about them on the Internet. We discovered them after photographing Hidden Falls on the Cascade River; we stopped and asked for directions from a very nice gentleman who was walking his dogs. He happily gave them to us, leading us right to the falls. When in doubt, ask a local!

Devil's Kettle, Brule River

A Minnesota mystery, Devil's Kettle gets its name because one of its twin falls mysteriously disappears. Despite all efforts to figure out where the water goes (and people have been trying for decades), it's still not clear where and how its water enters the lake.

Devil's Kettle, Brule River

A Minnesota must-see, Devil's Kettle boasts a fine pair of waterfalls, but many visitors come for the mystery of Devil's Kettle itself.

Location: Judge C. R. Magney State Park.

Address/GPS for the Falls: 4051 E Hwy. 61, Grand Marais, 55604; 47° 49'45.33" N, 90° 2'58.00" W.

Directions: 14 miles north of Grand Marais and 4 miles south of Hovland. Located near marker 124 on Hwy. 61.

Website: www.dnr.state.mn.us/state_parks/judge_cr_magney

Waterway: Brule River.

Nearest Town: Hovland.

Height: 50 feet. **Crest:** 40 feet wide when the whole river is flowing over the top; this occurs in May.

Hike Difficulty: Moderate to strenuous; there are many steps to deal with here.

Trail Quality: Good.

Round-trip Distance: 2 miles; plan on spending about 90 minutes to 2 hours to view Devil's Kettle and the Upper Falls.

Admission: A day pass at the state park is $5. A yearly vehicle pass is $25 and allows you to enter all state parks for a year.

Trip Report & Tips: Devil's Kettle wins the award for the most unique waterfall of them all. With the river splitting in half at the crest, the right waterfall plummets 50 feet down to the river bottom and the other half sinks down into a pothole. No one has ever figured out where it ends up. Dyed water and Ping-Pong balls have been sent down the raging kettle, never to be found again! If you go in May or after heavy spring run-off, you may not be able to view both falls; instead, they may be flowing as one huge, thundering waterfall.

To reach this bad boy, you must hike uphill for a mile. It was really tough the first time I hiked it, but the more and more I've visited Devil's Kettle, the easier the hike has become. You're going to start out by crossing the long green pedestrian bridge that crosses the bumpy Brule River. At 0.3 mile into your hike, you'll come to the first set of steps. There are only 21, so enjoy them. At this area you can sneak a peek down at the raging river rapids area. At 0.5 mile you'll come to the spur trail that will lead you down to the Lower Falls area (page 202). To get to the Devil's Kettle, you only need to travel 0.1 mile farther and you'll come to a beautiful vista with Upper Falls (page 180) off in the distance. There will also be two benches with your name on them. Sit a while and relax because you have a bunch of steps heading your way. After you're rested, keep going down the trail and trot down the 177 wooden steps. You'll head across the boardwalk and then see a sign that says "Devil's Kettle, 700 feet." Head up 57 more steps and, voilà, you've made it! You will not be disappointed with this monster at any season; it's raging in the spring, wild in the summer and stunning in the fall. If you want to get a closer look at the top of the pothole, head down from the viewing platform to a somewhat steep little trail. Here you can get right down to the river's edge by hugging a couple trees along the way, but be careful, as you really don't want to fall in. After you've enjoyed the falls, don't forget to stop at Upper Falls (page 180) on your return hike.

Portage Brook Falls

A jaw-dropping sight in spring, Portage Brook Falls is one of my all-around favorite falls on the North Shore.

I didn't know about this wonderful waterfall until my friend Sue and I went into the Chicago Bay Marketplace in Hovland for a quick lunch. The owner and a patron told us about this waterfall treasure; now it's one of my favorites on the North Shore.

Location: 13.1 miles north of Hovland on the Arrowhead Trail.

Address/GPS for the Falls: 47° 59'58.97" N, 90° 2'9.40" W.

Directions: Drive north on the Arrowhead Trail (Cook Cty. Rd. 16) for 12.4 miles. You'll see the Portage Brook overlook on the right; pass by it for now, but check it out later. It has great views, especially in the fall. Cross over the bridge and at 13.1 miles turn left on Shoe Lake Rd. and park in the grassy area on the left.

Website: None.

Waterway: Portage Brook.

Nearest Town: Hovland.

Height: 20 feet. **Crest:** 35 feet.

Hike Difficulty: Moderate. **Trail Quality:** Fair.

Round-trip Distance: 0.2 mile.

Admission: None.

Trip Report & Tips: When you get out of your vehicle, head back over the Arrowhead Trail; straight in front of you will be a narrow, well-worn trail. It heads down into the ditch and leads into the thick trees. Hike less than 0.1 mile down the skinny path through the thick evergreens to the falls. Along the way, you'll also cross downed birch trees as you head down to the river. As you get closer, things get steep, so it becomes something of a tree-hugger (you'll need to hang onto trees on your way down). Thankfully, it's much easier coming up.

The falls flow over a rocky ledge, plummet down about 20 feet and then tumble over three more layers of rock. If you visit the falls in May, when the water is really running, it will be a jaw-dropping sight; you'll want to bring towels to keep your gear dry and maybe even wear your rain boots. When we visited in May, Sue and I decided not to venture downstream with the water flowing so quickly.

If you go in September, you'll see a whole different waterfall. When I visited the falls in September, there were actually two falls present—the main falls and mini-waterfalls—as well as a cove that was clearly visible off to the left side.

It doesn't matter when you visit Portage Brook Falls, as it's truly a waterfall to seek out in all seasons.

Partridge Falls, Pigeon River

One of my "top five" falls on the North Shore, Partridge Falls is majestic, but getting there takes some effort.

A visit to these falls is an adventure, but what a reward you get once you reach your destination!

Location: Grand Portage Indian Reservation.

Address/GPS for the Falls: 47° 59'40.42" N, 89° 50'45.05" W.

Directions: If you are heading northeast on Hwy. 61 you'll want to take a left onto Old Hwy. 61. Drive 6.2 miles and stay left on Old Hwy. 61 for 2 more miles. Turn slightly left onto Partridge Falls Rd. for 4.3 miles. When the road splits, stay to the left all the way to the river. Allow a good 30 to 40 minutes for this bumpy ride. If you are coming from Grand Portage, turn right on Cty. Rd. 17, located by mile marker 143. Go 4 miles on Cty. Rd. 17, turn right on Cty. Rd. 89 and drive north 2 miles. Turn left on Partridge Falls Road and go 4.3 miles to the river.

Waterway: Pigeon River.

Nearest Town: Grand Portage.

Height: 30–40 feet. **Crest:** 70–80 feet.

Hike Difficulty: Moderate. **Trail Quality:** Poor.

Round-trip Distance: 0.4 mile.

Admission: None.

Trip Report & Tips: Partridge Falls is one of my favorite falls on the North Shore. It's also one that it takes some time and effort to reach, and while I highly recommend a visit, you also need to be very careful. The falls are located on Partridge Falls Rd., a minimum-maintenance road full of rocks and potholes. I highly suggest that you take a vehicle with four-wheel drive, as well as an extra tire, bottled water, and some snacks and sandwiches. (If you can do this trip toward the end of September, you'll be fine driving slowly because the view of fall colors will be amazing.)

The falls are located at the end of Partridge Falls Road. As you make it back to the end of the road and to the Pigeon River, park your vehicle and get ready for a short hike down a wide path. If it has just rained, you will need to dodge some wet spots in the low areas of the trail. As you are hiking along, you will soon hear the water roar. This is a great location to get a high-angle sneak peek of the falls. Next, you'll want to find the extremely steep rocky and mossy path that will bring you down to the riverside. Thankfully, there are many roots and small trees on the hike down, and you'll likely need to hang onto them for safety's sake. As you get closer to the bottom, you'll encounter an awesome side view of the falls, and if you stand in front of them, you may be showered in mist.

I was just amazed at how in-your-face these falls truly are. When you stand back to admire, you'll see that they are twice as wide as they are tall. The water flows out and over a bowed rocky face and pours over multiple jagged rocks with two spillways off to each side. This dramatic scenery makes the falls a great location for self portraits, as you're not going to find many places with a background like this one!

High Falls, Pigeon River

The highest waterfall in Minnesota, the High Falls of the Pigeon River is absolutely unforgettable at any time of year, and when water levels are up, the falls are simply sublime.

This is the highest waterfall in Minnesota and one of the best. If I lived in the area, this is a waterfall that I'd visit every day.

Location: Grand Portage State Park.

Address/GPS for the Falls: 9393 E Hwy. 61, Grand Portage, 55605; 48° 0'16.56" N, 89° 35'52.74" W.

Directions: Just south of the Ontario border near mile marker 150.

Website: www.dnr.state.mn.us/grandportage

Waterway: Pigeon River.

Nearest Town: Grand Portage.

Height: 92–120 feet (Ontario says 92 feet, Grand Portage State Park says 120 feet).

Crest: Varies greatly depending on season; can range from 20 feet to 200 feet.

Hike Difficulty: Easy. **Trail Quality:** Good.

Round-trip Distance: 1 mile on a paved trail that is handicapped accessible.

Admission: None. Even though the waterfalls are located on the grounds of the state park, a state park sticker is not needed to view the falls.

Trip Report & Tips: The hike back to High Falls is a short, easy 0.5-mile walk. These are easily among my top five favorite falls in the state. I like them so much because they never let me down, no matter the time of year. Whenever you visit, you're sure to be impressed by the sheer beauty and raging power of the falls.

Before you head out on your hike, check out the visitor center. They sometimes have recent video clips of the falls so you can see what they look like before you hike out there. Once you're ready to start, the paved trail is well marked, and once you see the wooden boardwalk you'll know that you are getting really close, as you'll be able to hear the falls. After a short walk on the boardwalk, 40 steps will lead you up to the far left-side viewing platform. Here you can get a closer look and actually see the magnitude of High Falls and just how much the white, silky water contrasts with the rock wall that the water is tumbling over.

The best overlook doesn't require any additional steps at all; it's actually at the end of the boardwalk and no stairs/steps are needed. As proof, I brought my mom out to view the falls. She doesn't handle steps and long walks too well, but I knew this would be a doable hike for her.

For another fine look at the falls, there are 17 steps at the end of the out-look to another vantage point.

When you go, you may want to bring a towel along because you could get wet, especially in the spring and early summer. Visiting in winter is another option, as only 25 people visit the park per day on average in winter, almost guaranteeing that you'll have the falls to yourself.

Location: Gooseberry Falls State Park.

Address/GPS for the Falls: 3206 Hwy. 61, Two Harbors, 55616; 47° 8'38.07" N, 91° 28'8.20" W.

Directions: 12 miles northeast of Two Harbors or 5 miles southwest of Split Rock Lighthouse at mile marker 39 on Hwy. 61.

Website: www.dnr.state.mn.us/state_parks/gooseberry_falls/

Waterway: Gooseberry River.

Height: 30–40 feet. **Crest:** 30–35 feet wide at the top; the bottom of the falls fans out to around 70 feet.

Nearest Town: Two Harbors.

Hike Difficulty: Easy. **Trail Quality:** Good.

Round-trip Distance: The distance really depends on how much hiking around the park you do. If you just go to the falls and back, it's a little less than 0.5 mile, round trip. Then again, you're so close to the Middle and Lower Falls that you probably want to see those too.

Admission: A day pass at the state park is $5. A yearly vehicle pass is $25 and allows you to enter all state parks for a year.

Trip Report & Tips: Starting from the Visitor Center, take the mostly paved Falls Loop Trail toward the Gateway Plaza. Follow the walkway under the Hwy. 61 bridge, and there you'll see beautiful Upper Falls. There are great vantage points around much of the falls. If you keep hiking along the trail, you'll eventually be standing above the falls. For an easy-to-moderate 2-mile hike, keep hiking upriver, where you'll see Fifth Falls, along with some very cool rock formations.

Also, consider visiting the Upper Falls in winter. The Upper Falls Trail is maintained in the winter. If you do visit, bring anti-slip traction cleats to put over your boots; you'll need them!

Location: Gooseberry Falls State Park.

Address/GPS for the Falls: 3206 Hwy. 61, Two Harbors, 55616; 47° 8'34.85" N, 91° 28'4.04" W.

Directions: 12 miles northeast of Two Harbors or 5 miles southwest of Split Rock Lighthouse at mile marker 39 on Hwy. 61.

Website: www.dnr.state.mn.us/state_parks/gooseberry_falls/

Waterway: Gooseberry River.

Height: 25 feet. **Crest:** Around 40 feet, but can vary dramatically based on the time of year.

Nearest Town: Two Harbors.

Hike Difficulty: Good. **Trail Quality:** Easy. The Falls Loop Trail is paved most of the way with some boardwalk areas and a few steps.

Round-trip Distance: 1 mile for Lower and Middle Falls, although it really depends on how much hiking you do around the falls. You can make this a quick trip or a lengthy one.

Trip Report & Tips: The Middle Falls at Gooseberry are large and can be positively massive at times of high water flow. They are also a lot of fun to photograph during any season. The Falls Loop Trail goes all the way around both sides of the Middle and Lower Falls, enabling you to see them at different levels. On the west side of the river, you'll find a boardwalk and steps bringing you downstream to a footbridge. This is one of my favorite areas to photograph the Lower and Middle Falls together. Head across the bridge over to the east side of the river for a more rugged trail and great views from higher up. As the Middle Falls flow down over their very long, rocky ledge, look for the large "rock island" before the river plummets to the Lower Falls.

This is another falls to consider visiting in winter, as you're likely to see wildlife (especially white-tailed deer), and the falls are otherworldly when covered in ice. If you visit in winter, make sure you wear proper footwear (traction-control ice cleats). The steps will have packed snow and the walkways can be very slippery with large amounts of ice during the spring.

Location: Split Rock Wayside Rest.

Address/GPS for the Falls: 47° 11'14.62" N, 91° 24'51.97" W.

Directions: At mile marker 43 on Hwy. 61 about 17 miles northeast of Two Harbors.

Website: None.

Waterway: Split Rock River.

Height: 20 feet. **Crest:** Varies.

Nearest Town: Beaver Bay.

Hike Difficulty: Easy. **Trail Quality:** Good.

Round-trip Distance: 1 mile.

Admission: None.

Trip Report & Tips: You'll find ample parking space at the Split Rock Wayside Rest. As you start up the path from the parking lot, you'll pass by some large stacked rocks and some signage explaining the name of the river. To reach the falls, follow the Split Rock Loop Trail. After a half mile into your hike you will head down some steps and come to a pedestrian bridge and the falls area. Either view the falls from the bridge or carefully head down to the water's edge for a closer look. Needless to say, the scenery is idyllic, and it's pretty easy to lose track of time in this hidden and very secluded area. My friend Sue and I ventured back to the falls on a beautiful Sunday morning in mid-May. The first hikers we met warned us of some wolves ahead. Yikes! Thankfully, we did not meet up with the furry little fellas. If you're feeling adventurous, there are nine more waterfalls located up the river, if you want to make the moderate 4-mile round-trip hike.

Location: Beaver Bay.

Address/GPS for the Falls: 47° 15'39.05" N, 91° 17'48.39" W.

Directions: Located near mile marker 51 on Hwy. 61 northeast of Beaver Bay. Either park near the Hwy. 61 bridge or turn on Lax Lake Rd. and park in the paved parking lot next to the river.

Website: None.

Waterway: Beaver River.

Height: The river flows down with multiple cascades and waterfalls dropping about 300 total feet. **Crest:** Varies.

Nearest Town: Beaver Bay.

Hike Difficulty: Easy from bridge; moderate down to river. **Trail Quality:** Great up on the bridge; poor down to the river.

Round-trip Distance: Less than 0.1 mile when you view from bridge; 0.3 mile if you hike down and around at river level.

Admission: None.

Trip Report & Tips: Don't we all love a huge waterfall that can be seen from the road? Easily accessible from the sidewalk on the Hwy. 61 bridge, this waterfall is situated among lovely scenery, and if you're a photography lover, you'll find many ways to compose your images. If you want a closer look, venture down the crazy-steep trail to the river's edge and enjoy the unparalleled up-close views. Before you do, however, take stock of the river's current. If the water is running really fast, use caution or just enjoy the view from afar.

The main falls cover a huge, flat expanse of rock, and the smaller falls fan out and flow down a couple hundred of feet, then run smack into a huge round rock. This splits the river in two, forming two more large cascades of water. In my experience, Beaver River Falls looks its best during spring run-off or in the fall surrounded by changing colors of the area maples and birches.

Location: Off of Hwy. 61 in Beaver Bay.

Address/GPS for the Falls: 47° 16'2.61" N, 91° 17'58.57" W.

Directions: From Hwy. 61 in Beaver Bay, turn north on Lax Lake Rd. (Co. Rd. 4) and go 0.7 mile. Park in the Superior Hiking Trail lot on your right.

Website: None.

Waterway: Beaver River.

Height: 20 feet. **Crest:** Varies.

Nearest Town: Beaver Bay.

Hike Difficulty: Moderate. **Trail Quality:** Fair.

Round-trip Distance: 1.8 miles.

Admission: None.

Trip Report & Tips: From the parking lot, head to your right and down the gravel road. After a few minutes you will come to a brown suspension footbridge that crosses over the Beaver River. Cross the bridge and take an immediate right onto Superior Hiking Trail. It will follow along the river. You will pass by the north Beaver River campsite and cross a few boards around the muddy spots. At 0.8 mile, you'll head up a hill and pass by South Beaver River campsite before going downhill. The river will be getting more turbulent as you go. At 0.9 mile you'll see the South Camp Falls roaring amid the black lava rock. If you visit the falls in mid-May, the water will be wild and the rocks will be wet. If you try to get a closer look under such conditions, be careful since you will have to do some scrambling to get a better look at the falls.

My friend Sue and I spent an hour and a half on our South Camp Falls adventure. It started to pour while we were out photographing the falls. If rain is in the forecast, be sure to pack rain gear and a skinny umbrella; wide umbrellas won't fit through all the trees on this trail. Also, if there is heavy rain, this part of the Superior Hiking Trail quickly becomes waterlogged, so bring your boots!

Location: Outside Beaver Bay.

Address/GPS for the Falls: 47° 15'55.18" N, 91° 20'36.58" W.

Directions: Turn off Hwy. 61 in Beaver Bay onto Lax Lake Rd. (Cty. Rd. 4) and head north 1.6 miles. Next, you'll want to turn left and drive 1.2 miles on Cty. Rd. 3. You'll see a little dirt road on the left. It gets a bit rough, so be careful where you park. You may want to take the truck to this one or park on the side of the road. It's a short hike to the river.

Website: None.

Waterway: Beaver River.

Height: Varies from 2 feet to 8 feet. **Crest:** Varies significantly depending on location; can be as wide as the river.

Nearest Town: Beaver Bay.

Hike Difficulty: Easy. **Trail Quality:** Good, although there really isn't a trail; just park and head out to the river.

Round-trip Distance: 0.1 mile, depending on how much exploring you do around the river. If water levels are lower, you can trudge through the river for a little more fun and adventure.

Admission: None.

Trip Report & Tips: This hidden gem cannot be seen from the road, but every time I've visited these falls it's been great. It doesn't matter if the water level is high or low, the falls are always fun and interesting. In the spring you'll find a wild, wide and raging river, and getting close to the river or rock-hopping will be out of the question. In the fall, you'll find a river with an entirely different personality. Part of the area's appeal stems from the many tall pines and crazy cedar trees that grow near the falls; these give the falls a unique character all year long. The actual falls are often quite wide and flow steeply down the bedrock, leaving many rapids and miniature falls in their wake. When you visit, wear your boots because you can capture some great images if the water is low enough to allow you to trek into the water safely.

- **Location:** Tettegouche State Park.

Address/GPS for the Falls: 47° 21'31.72" N, 91° 12'50.23" W.

Directions: Off of Hwy. 61 by mile marker 59, turn on Hwy. 1 and go north 1.5 miles to a small gravel parking area on the left-hand side; it's located by two yellow state park signs.

Website: www.dnr.state.mn.us/state_parks/tettegouche/index.html

Waterway: Baptism River.

Height: 29 feet. **Crest:** Varies.

Nearest Town: Finland.

Hike Difficulty: Easy. **Trail Quality:** Good.

Round-trip Distance: 0.2 mile.

Admission: None; though if you plan on accessing the state park, you'll need to purchase a day pass for your vehicle for $5.

Trip Report & Tips: From the parking lot, head down the well-worn path by the state park sign. Go downhill, pass by the Illgen Falls cabin, and walk across the boardwalk and the 35 steps down to the top of the falls. If you want to avoid the stairs, you get a fine view of the falls from the boardwalk, but you'll need a wide-angle or fish-eye lens to capture the whole scene. If you plan on heading to the edge of the rock, make sure you have proper footwear; on my trip, my sandals slipped, so I quickly took them off and went barefoot. If you choose to head down closer to the river level, you can climb down, but if you do, be careful, as it's very steep and you're high up from the river.

Once you're done exploring the falls, check out the rest of the park. It features rugged, semi-mountainous terrain that's interspersed with waterfalls, inland lakes and a mile of Lake Superior shoreline, more than enough to explore.

Location: The mouth of the Manitou River.

Address/GPS for the Falls: 47° 26'34.55" N, 91° 3'52.63" W.

Directions: Only accessible by boat.

Website: We opted to go with Tofte Charters; www.toftecharters.com

Waterway: Manitou River.

Height: 35–40 feet. **Crest:** 8–10 feet.

Nearest Town: Little Marais.

Hike Difficulty: No hike is available; you have to see this from a boat.

Trail Quality: See above.

Round-trip Distance: 18 miles by boat, kayak or canoe from Taconite Harbor.

Admission: Varies by charter service.

Trip Report & Tips: Since the land around the falls is privately owned, the mouth of the Manitou River is only accessible by boat. As most charter services are dedicated to fishing, you can't be totally set on a date because it depends on both the fishing schedule and the area weather. We initially wanted to visit in September, but weather made that impossible, so we set out from Taconite Harbor on a beautiful, cool May morning. Our charter service of choice was Tofte Charters with Captain Darren Peck. Darren has a wealth of information about the North Shore and the lake. On the way over to Manitou Falls, we headed by the mouth of the Caribou River, Last Creek Falls, Sugarloaf Cove and some amazing Lake Superior homes, including a glass house. We also drifted over portions of an old sunken schooner-barge called the *Amboy* near Taconite Harbor. It went aground and sank in the Mataafa Storm of 1905.

As we approached the high cliffs surrounding the falls, Darren slowly cruised into the somewhat secluded bay. The falls come down in their own little circular cove, and when you get closer, you'll see an awesome arch off to the side that kayakers paddle under. It's definitely worth the extra effort to see this natural wonder.

Location: Two miles south of Schroeder, just north of Taconite Harbor near mile marker 77 on Hwy. 61.

Address/GPS for the Falls: 47° 31'38.23" N, 90° 55'52.28" W.

Directions: Drive into a narrow gravel driveway just south of Two Island River. It's on the left-hand (west) side. You can park your vehicle in the small parking area that's 0.1 mile down the road and hike the 0.3 mile up to the second set of railroad tracks. You can also drive up the narrow, minimum-maintenance road for a total of 0.4 mile. I chose not to drive because I didn't want my SUV to get scratched.

Website: None.

Waterway: Two Island River.

Height: 40 feet. **Crest:** 20 feet.

Nearest Town: Schroeder.

Hike Difficulty: Easy. **Trail Quality:** Good.

Round-trip Distance: 0.8 mile if you hike from small parking area; 0.6 if you drive to the railroad tracks and walk to the falls.

Admission: None.

Trip Report & Tips: It's an easy walk up the 0.3-mile minimum-maintenance road. The road meanders a bit but eventually meets a set of railroad tracks. Hike up the ditch, cross the tracks (though be mindful of passing trains), and you'll then see beautiful Upper Two Island River Falls off to your left. (The cascading 40-foot falls are absolutely gorgeous in the fall.) This is a picture-perfect spot to get your waterfall photos. After you capture some images, head down the grassy path for a closer look at this hidden gem. I ran into two fly fishermen while at the falls. They told me there were more waterfalls up above this one; a hike up either side of the falls will bring you to three more falls, which I informally dubbed the "Triple Falls" (page 194).

Location: Cross River Falls Wayside.

Address/GPS for the Falls: 7932 Hwy. 61, Schroeder, 55613. This is the address for the Cross River Heritage Center, located right next to the falls; 47° 32'39.16" N, 90° 53'48.36" W.

Directions: You can see the upper portion of the falls from the Hwy. 61 bridge in Schroeder. It's located at Hwy. 61 mile marker 79, across from the Cross River Heritage Center.

Website: www.crossriverheritage.org

Waterway: Cross River.

Height: Gradually slopes for 200–300 feet. **Crest:** 40 feet upper, 20 feet lower.

Nearest Town: Schroeder.

Hike Difficulty: It's easy to view the Upper Falls; just stand on the bridge. It's strenuous going down to the Lower Falls under the bridge; you'll need to make your way down there, and you'll likely need to grab a tree or some roots for support.

Trail Quality: Great on the bridge; poor going down to the Lower Falls.

Round-trip Distance: 0.3 mile.

Admission: None.

Trip Report & Tips: If you're viewing from the bridge, the falls are about 40 feet across and slope down 100-plus feet before they disappear under the bridge. Once you've photographed the bridge view of the falls, you need to decide if you want to embark upon the short, but challenging, hike to the Lower Falls. If you opt to do so, head across Hwy. 61 and either go down about 37 steps to a poor viewing area, or head down one of two steep paths down to the river level. (These paths are tricky; you may even need to slide down.) When I visited, the river was really flowing beneath the bridge and the falls were tossing and turning down the narrow gorge. At the base of the falls, look for a huge indentation in the rock carved out by years of flowing water. Eventually the water from the falls enters a large pool-like area before cascading over even more rocks, turning to the east and finally heading down into Lake Superior.

Temperance River Falls

Location: Temperance River State Park.

Address/GPS for the Falls: 7620 West Highway 61, Schroeder, 55613.

Directions: Located at mile marker 80 on Hwy 61; you'll see parking on both sides of the highway by the Temperance River Bridge.

Website: www.dnr.state.mn.us/state_parks/temperance_river

Waterway: Temperance River.

Height: Lower Temperance River Falls, Slopes down about 20 feet **Hidden Falls,** 15 feet, **Bridge Falls,** Varies **Mighty Rock Falls,** 20 feet **Crashing Water Falls,** 15 feet **Namaste Falls,** 10 feet **Upper Falls,** Varies.

Crest: Lower Temperance River Falls, Varies **Hidden Falls,** Varies **Bridge Falls,** Varies **Mighty Rock Falls,** 20 feet **Crashing Water Falls,** 12 feet **Namaste Falls,** 35 feet **Upper Falls,** 50 feet.

Nearest Town: Schroeder.

Hike Difficulty: It's a moderate hike with lots of stops along the way to view the falls. Make sure you have good tread on your shoes.

Trail Quality: Good, but keep children at hand and your dog on a leash. To view all the waterfalls, you will be very close to the edge of the steep gorge, so be cautious.

Round-trip Distance: 0.6 mile if you go all the way to Namaste Falls.

Admission: Free, but if you park in the state park, you'll need a $5 day pass.

Trip Report & Tips: Start out by admiring the Lower Temperance River Falls, which is visible from just feet away from the parking area. To begin your hike to the other falls, head to the northwest corner of the parking lot, and hike down the Gorge Trail, which is a spur trail off of the Superior Hiking Trail. Stay on the path on the northeast side of the river. It's only a short 0.1-mile hike to Hidden Falls, which falls about 15 feet then winds around a bit and tumbles down another 5 feet. It is really tucked back in the gorge and challenging to photograph. After Hidden Falls you'll encounter 39 old stone steps that will take you up to higher viewing areas. The next area you'll want to go peek at is the cauldron. It is behind Hidden Falls (upstream) and also

(continued on page 171)

Hidden Falls

Bridge Falls

Mighty Rock Falls

Crashing Water Falls

Namaste Falls

Upper Falls

Trip Report (continued): a bit challenging to photograph but cool to sneak a look at. Not too much farther up the rock base is Bridge Falls, which is located under the first brown pedestrian bridge. Here, the Temperance River flows down and is pinched between the rocks, forcing it through this skinny crack in the deep gorge. Take time to roam around here and check everything out, as this area has some amazing rock formations, and it's one of the most unique places on the North Shore. After you're done exploring, keep heading up the trail following the river. The next waterfall you'll encounter I've dubbed Mighty Rock Falls. When you see it, you'll know why. It's about 20 feet high and 20 feet wide. The river comes around a 90-degree curve from the south and heads east. To the right of the falls is a mighty rock that has been chiseled by the raging water over the years. The falls can be nicely viewed from afar, or you can get a closer look from the viewing platform and even hike up on top of the mighty rock and look down on the falling water. If you opt to do this, be careful, as there are no guard-rails up there. If you keep heading upriver, you'll encounter Crashing Water Falls, which is exactly 15 feet high, 12 feet wide and features a very nice large viewing area with a rock wall so you don't fall over the edge. The last falls you'll see on this hike we named Namaste Falls, which features huge basalt slabs where you can sit and reflect. It's also a great place to dip your feet in the water or to sit and read a book. Namaste Falls is about 35 feet wide and 10 feet high. From there, you can head back the way you came, admiring each falls again as you pass by.

If you're hungry for more waterfalls, drive to the Upper Temperance River Falls. To get there by car, leave the parking lot and go south 0.1 mile and turn right on Temperance Road. Go 0.7 mile up the gravel road and park in the mid-sized parking lot on the right. From the parking area, head down the trail toward the river. Start off your hike with 38 steps and take the path to the left. At 0.3 miles you will reach the Upper Falls. The top of the falls area is about 50 feet wide and cascades down to your right.

Lower Falls, Poplar River

Location: Southwest of Lutsen.

Address/GPS for the Falls: 5700 W Hwy. 61, Lutsen, 55612; 47° 38'13.49" N, 90° 42'26.02" W.

Directions: From Lutsen, head south on Hwy. 61; near mile marker 90, you'll see the huge Lutsen Resort sign. Drive into the Lutsen Resort driveway; loop around the hotel and park your vehicle on the east side of the building in the parking lot.

Website: lutsenresort.com

Waterway: Poplar River.

Height: 15 feet. **Crest:** Varies.

Nearest Town: Lutsen.

Hike Difficulty: Easy. **Trail Quality:** Good.

Round-trip Distance: It's a very short distance to everything; it just depends on how much exploring you want to do.

Admission: None, but support the folks at Lutsen if you can.

Trip Report & Tips: From the parking lot, head over to either of the old covered pedestrian bridges. You will see great views of the falls from both bridges. The main falls flow over from the top bridge and cascade to the lower bridge. Roam down to the mouth of the river and explore Lutsen's huge beach area. One of the times I visited, the huge waves were splashing up against the rocks. When I was photographing, it was challenging and fun to time it just right to capture that big splash against the rock. Take your time here; you may even want to stay a few nights. It's a very scenic and fun area to explore, and you'll find time passes quite quickly.

One of the beautiful advantages of the Poplar River Valley is that it's especially pretty and picturesque when it's overcast, and it can look very dramatic if it's raining and the rocks are wet.

Location: Cascade River State Park.

Address/GPS for the Falls: 3481 W Hwy. 61, Lutsen, 55612; 47° 42'34.95" N, 90° 31'26.66" W.

Directions: Located at mile marker 100 on Hwy. 61. It is 10 miles north of Lutsen and 9 miles south of Grand Marais.

Website: www.dnr.state.mn.us/state_parks/cascade_river

Waterway: Cascade River.

Height: Each cascading waterfall plummets 5–20 feet with the one closest to the viewing platform dropping the most. **Crest:** Varies.

Nearest Town: Grand Marais.

Hike Difficulty: Fair. **Trail Quality:** Moderate; the trail gets tougher as you go.

Round-trip Distance: 0.4 mile.

Admission: Parking off of Hwy. 61 is free, but if you plan on venturing into the park proper, you'll need to buy a $5 day pass.

Trip Report & Tips: There is ample parking at mile marker 100 near the Cascade River. Look for the sign that says "Cascade Falls 300 feet" and head up a few rock steps on the well-worn path that will lead you right to Cascade Falls. To view the Cascades, continue on the path that goes to the left of Cascade Falls. There, you'll encounter a wooden guardrail, 34 wooden steps and a boardwalk, as well as a wooden overlook at the top of Cascade Falls. Turn around from the viewing platform and head down a few rocky steps to view some smaller, yet very pretty, cascades. This area is especially beautiful in late afternoon and early evening. Head back up to the trail and go about five minutes farther to see the Cascades. You'll head up 42 more steps, eventually coming to a bridge and the Cascades viewing area. The bridge is a great place to photograph the two lower portions of the Cascades. You'll also see a sign explaining why the river's water is root beer colored and find another picture-perfect viewing area. If you continue up the trail to the left of the river and head down the spur trails, you'll see the huge boulder that splits the river, forming the two top falls of the Cascades.

Lower Falls, Fall River

Location: Just south of Grand Marais.

Address/GPS for the Falls: 47° 44'29.36" N, 90° 23'17.65" W.

Directions: Mile marker 107 on Hwy. 61 just 2 miles south of Grand Marais.

Website: None.

Waterway: Fall River, which is also known as Rosebush Creek.

Height: 33 feet. **Crest:** 11 feet.

Nearest Town: Grand Marais.

Hike Difficulty: Moderate. **Trail Quality:** Poor.

Round-trip Distance: 0.2 mile.

Admission: None.

Trip Report & Tips: To get to this waterfall, you'll have to park along the side of the road on Hwy. 61 near mile marker 107. Once you've done so, find the path on the Lake Superior side. This trail is a bit strenuous; it can be wet and muddy, so I wouldn't bring kids. After a couple minutes of hiking, you'll be at the falls, which are situated on a high cliff that's not protected with any guardrails. My friend Sue and I visited the falls in mid-May and it was simply awesome. The water falls straight down into a large pool that is semi-enclosed by jagged red rock walls. If the water levels are lower, you can even venture down to the Lake Superior shore for more exploring. When the water levels are very low, you can also check out the top of the falls by walking through the culvert from the other side of the highway, though exercise caution if you opt to do this and don't attempt it if the water is flowing quickly.

Location: The Kadunce River Wayside.

Address/GPS for the Falls: 47° 48'1.90" N, 90° 9'26.40" W.

Directions: To reach the Kadunce River Wayside (also spelled Kodonce) head to mile marker 118.7 on Hwy. 61. It is located just 8 miles northeast of Grand Marais.

Website: None.

Waterway: Kadunce River.

Height: At the top it drops 4 feet, then there is a 14-foot slope down and the bottom drop is 6.5 feet. **Crest:** Varies.

Nearest Town: Colvill.

Hike Difficulty: Moderate to strenuous if you head down the steep area to falls at river level; otherwise it's fairly easy hiking. **Trail Quality:** Good to fair; there are some steps, roots and rocks to hike over.

Round-trip Distance: 2 miles to view most of the falls.

Admission: None.

Trip Report & Tips: From the wayside parking lot, cross over Hwy. 61 and look for the Superior Hiking Trail sign. Start hiking up alongside the river, then go up 21 wooden steps. After you've walked 0.2 mile, you'll see a sign that reads "Don't throw rocks into the gorge," which marks the area for "Tree Hugger Falls" (page 200). After a few more minutes into your hike, you'll hear the water roaring off to your left. Look for a clearing and you'll find Heart of the Earth Falls, a good-sized waterfall that flows down in the deep red canyon and takes a 90-degree turn to tumble down even farther. To view these falls from the river level, you'll want to start hiking down in the river after about 0.7 mile into your hike. Be very careful. When my friend Jessica and I explored the Kadunce River, we came down on the top of Heart of the Earth Falls and then carefully scaled down the steep, large rocks to get down to the bottom of the falls. We were there in September when the water levels were lower and we could actually walk across the river. A visit would be an entirely different story in May or after a storm when water levels are fierce.

Location: Judge C. R. Magney State Park.

Address/GPS for the Falls: 4051 E Hwy. 61, Grand Marais, 55604; 47° 49'40.42" N, 90° 2'52.85" W.

Directions: Near mile marker 124 on Hwy. 61. 14 miles north of Grand Marais and 4 miles south of Hovland.

Website: www.dnr.state.mn.us/state_parks/judge_cr_magney/index.html

Waterway: Brule River.

Height: 20 feet. **Crest:** 40 feet.

Nearest Town: Hovland.

Hike Difficulty: Moderate. **Trail Quality:** Good.

Round-trip Distance: 2 miles.

Admission: A day pass at the state park is $5. A yearly vehicle pass is $25 and allows you to enter all state parks for a year.

Trip Report & Tips: From the state park's parking lot, you'll hike 0.9 mile and you'll see 21 metal steps heading down to your right. Take those down to the river and bring a towel along. If it's spring, you're guaranteed to get sprayed. If you need a cold shower, then this is the place for you. The first time I visited, it was sunny out and there was a huge bright rainbow going across the whole falls, so I nicknamed it "Rainbow Falls." You can get a few different vantage points down here. One is off to the side, you just have to move around a bit since there is a big boulder blocking your view. If you want to hike downriver a bit, creep through the woods for about 60 feet and find yourself a big rock to perch upon. You should be able to find one to set your gear on and then you don't have to worry about getting wet. You may also want to wear some waterproof boots, but I usually wear my lightweight tennis shoes to this one for easier travel on all the steps. Heading back from Upper Falls, you'll have the 21 metal steps and the 177 wooden steps to tackle before heading back to the parking lot.

Location: Pigeon River Provincial Park in Ontario, Canada.

Address/GPS for the Falls: 48° 0'48.94" N, 89° 36'56.10" W.

Directions: Cross the U.S.-Canada border (have your passport ready). After leaving the crossing, head out on Hwy. 61 north; the Ontario Visitor Center is not far from the crossing, and they have a great informational center as well as restrooms. Once you're on your way, go 1.5 miles north on Hwy. 61, and then turn left and go southwest 0.9 mile on Route 593 to the Pigeon River Provincial Park parking lot.

Website: www.ontarioparks.com/park/pigeonriver

Waterway: Pigeon River.

Height: The Lower Middle Falls are 15–20 feet high; the Upper Middle Falls are 4 feet, and cascade down another 8 feet to the bottom falls. **Crest:** Lower Middle Falls are very wide, about 50 feet. The crest of the upper middle falls varies.

Nearest U.S. Town: Grand Portage, Minnesota.

Hike Difficulty: Easy. **Trail Quality:** Good.

Round-trip Distance: If you walk, it's a round trip of 0.9 mile; if you drive to both areas to view the falls, you'll only walk about 0.1 mile.

Admission: None, but you'll need your passport.

Trip Report & Tips: For more adventure, head to Canada's Pigeon River Provincial Park. At the parking lot you can either park your vehicle and hike 0.25 mile to the falls, or get back on Route 593 and drive 0.3 mile, where you'll see Lower Middle Falls on your left. If you drive, get out and hike over to the river for a great view of Lower Middle Falls. Drive about 0.1 mile farther up the hill and park at the top of the hill by the curve. Look for the skinny, well-packed trail that heads through the pine trees. This will lead you to a big rock that sits about 10 feet above Lower Middle Falls. It's a little bit steep heading down to the rock, so be careful. This is one of my top five favorite spots to sit and reflect; too bad it's 324 miles from my home.

Please note: This waterfall is also accessible via a trail at Grand Portage State Park in Minnesota.

Orange Fal

Location: On the Superior Hiking Trail at Split Rock Wayside Rest.

Address/GPS for the Falls: First Falls: 47°11'23.25" N, 91°25'1.29" W. (See trip report for directions to the others.)

Directions: At mile marker 43 on Hwy. 61 about 17 miles northeast of Two Harbors. There's ample parking at the wayside rest.

Website: None.

Waterway: Split Rock River.

Height: First Falls, 20 feet **White Falls,** 30–35 feet **Two-Step Falls,** Left side, 35 feet; right side, 10–15 feet **Red Falls,** 15–20 feet **The Slide,** 10–15 feet **The Upper Slide Falls,** 15–20 feet **Island Falls**, Varies **Split Rock Falls,** Varies **Orange Falls,** 5 feet.

Crest: **First Falls,** 60 feet **White Falls,** 60 feet **Two-Step Falls,** 35–40 feet **Red Falls,** 35–40 feet **The Slide**, 40–50 feet **The Upper Slide Falls,** 40–50 feet **Island Falls,** Varies **Split Rock Falls,** 30–40 feet **Orange Falls** 8 feet.

Nearest U.S. Town: Beaver Bay.

Hike Difficulty: Moderate. **Trail Quality:** Fair to poor.

Round-trip Distance: 4 miles if you visit all 9 falls.

Admission: None.

Trip Report & Tips: Now it's time for something a little different. The following *nine* waterfalls are all found, one after another, along the Superior Hiking Trail. They offer a dizzying amount of variety, and a hike to all nine, while strenuous, is well worth it. (Of course, so is a hike just to one or two!) To reach the First Falls, named First Falls, appropriately enough, follow the Split Rock Loop Trail of the Superior Hiking Trail. You'll encounter a bridge at the west branch of the Split Rock River, and you'll need to hike up 32 steps. At 0.7 mile into your hike, you'll start to hear the falls, which are located by a double-plank bridge. Please use extreme caution in this area; it is very steep down to the river. Just 10 minutes past First Falls, you come to the biggest waterfall on this tour: White Falls. As you are hiking down the trail, you will first see it in the distance. This is a great vantage point for a picture since it's very difficult to see the whole falls as you get closer.

(continued on page 187)

First Falls

White Falls

Two-Step Falls

Red Falls

The Slide

The Upper Slide Falls

Island Falls

Split Rock Falls

Orange Falls

Trip Report (continued): As you continue on the trail, you'll pass by the falls from a higher elevation, but the view will be partially obstructed by trees. If you're hungry for more falls, keep hiking a few more minutes and you'll come to Two-Step Falls. Here, the river doesn't quite know which way to go, taking two wild turns. After only 0.2 mile from Two-Step Falls you'll come to a U-shaped curve in the trail and a wooden bridge that crosses over a small stream. By 1.4 miles the trail is at river level, though it soon rises and you'll see Red Falls off in the distance. Follow the sign that reads "Spur Trail to Overlook" and be sure to head out on the red rock outcrop at the river's edge for a great view. From the Red Falls spur trail you have a short and steep hike up to a partially blocked view of The Slide. To get there, you need to climb up about 41 crazy steps made up of roots and railroad ties. As you are high up on the trail, notice how the river slides to the left and the falls plummet down about 15–20 feet. A very short distance from The Slide, you will see The Upper Slide off in the distance. Keep hiking until you come to the large red rock outcropping at the top of the falls. From The Upper Slide, hike for a very short distance and you'll see Island Falls, one of my favorite falls. This falls is best viewed from the perfect perch point located right on the trail. In front of you will be two falls split by a huge red rock, forming an island. If you're not tapped out yet, begin your steep descent down to Split Rock Falls, which is 0.1 mile beyond Island Falls. When you find the pillars (two tall pink and red rhyolite stones), you'll know you're in the right place and you'll see a tiered, cascading waterfall flowing among tall red canyon walls and cedar trees. If you are hungry for one more waterfall, keep hiking just a short distance beyond the split rocks and you'll see Orange Falls. This is one of the more unique waterfalls of the bunch, as it travels down a skinny path and winds up in the wide Split Rock River. As you might expect, the rocks here have an orange cast to them. This is a great place to sit, relax and enjoy the view. You deserve it since you've just completed two rugged miles of hiking. From Orange Falls you can head back the 2 miles you hiked; the trip back to the wayside rest took about an hour.

French River Falls

Location: Off of the Hwy. 61 Expressway north of Duluth.

Address/GPS for the Falls: 46° 54'8.24" N, 91° 53'59.36" W.

Directions: Between mile marker 11 and 12 on the Hwy. 61 Expressway, north of Duluth. Pull off on Ryan Rd. (Cty. Rd. 50) to the left (west) and park on the edge of the road.

Website: None.

Waterway: French River.

Height: A series of falls totaling 35–40 feet.

Crest: 15 feet.

Nearest Town: Duluth.

Hike Difficulty: Fair.

Trail Quality: You'll be walking in the ditch.

Round-trip Distance: < 0.1 mile.

Admission: None.

Trip Report & Tips: Walk a short distance through the ditch of Hwy. 61 over to the French river. Carefully find your viewing location on the jagged black rocks located below the guard rail on the Hwy. 61 Expressway. You'll see as the river comes around the corner it has two 3–5 foot falls cascading to a pool area. Then it heads down a 45-degree slope for about 30 feet before it reaches another pool and heads under Hwy. 61. Note: The flow of the falls varies quite a bit with the seasons and rainfall.

Train Trestle Falls

Location: Between mile marker 11 and 12 on the Hwy. 61 Expressway north of Duluth.

Address/GPS for the Falls: 46° 54'5.29"N, 91° 53'49.05"W.

Directions: From Hwy. 61, pull off on Ryan Rd. (Cty. Rd. 50) to the right and park in the small parking lot just off the expressway. The lot will be on your left.

Website: None.

Waterway: French River.

Height: 4 feet. **Crest:** 8–10 feet.

Nearest Town: Duluth.

Hike Difficulty: Fair.

Trail Quality: You'll be walking in the ditch.

Round-trip Distance: 0.3 mile.

Admission: None.

Trip Report & Tips: The French River heads down toward Lake Superior with multiple Cascades and short waterfalls. There is a cute little 4-foot triple-tiered waterfall just before the train trestle bridge. To get to the bridge, walk a very short distance down Ryan Rd. and turn left at the railroad tracks. Walk alongside the tracks in the ditch over to the bridge to view the falls. Please remember to always use caution along the tracks and keep a safe distance from them. You can view the falls from up above or find a path down the steep embankment to the riverside. After the bridge the river cascades downstream to form some fun swimming holes and more falls.

Fifth Falls, Gooseberry River

Location: Gooseberry Falls State Park.

Address/GPS for the Falls: 3206 Hwy. 61, Two Harbors, 55616; 47° 8'53.58" N, 91° 28'34.85" W.

Directions: 12 miles north of Two Harbors at mile marker 39.

Website: www.dnr.state.mn.us/state_parks/gooseberry_falls/index.html

Waterway: Gooseberry River.

Height: The falls by the bridge cascade down around 10 feet; the Lower Falls are about 15–20 feet high.

Crest: Greatly depends on water levels of the river.

Nearest Town: Two Harbors.

Hike Difficulty: Easy to moderate.

Trail Quality: Good to fair.

Round-trip Distance: 2.2 miles.

Admission: A day pass at the state park is $5 and a yearly pass is $25.

Trip Report & Tips: From the visitor center, take the paved path to the Upper Falls area. From there, walk around to the left of Upper Falls and head back onto the Fifth Falls Trail, which takes you along the river. At 0.6 mile into your hike, you'll come to 43 stone steps that will take you up above the river. A little bit farther, at 0.7 mile, head downward on the trail as it follows the river. The trail gets a little bit more rugged here, and you'll later need to climb some stone steps. At the top of the trail is a log shelter decorated with carved names. Immediately after the trail shelter you'll get a high-angle view of Fifth Falls. Just before the shelter you can head down to the river for a view of the falls, and after the trail shelter, consider hiking to the bridge and crossing it. Then, pick up a spur trail that leads down to the rocky river's edge, which is perfect for photographing the falls. For your return hike back to the visitor center, choose the trail on the other side of the river for different scenery.

Two-Step Falls, Baptism River

Location: Tettegouche State Park.

Address/GPS for the Falls: 5702 Hwy. 61, Silver Bay, 55614; 47° 20'52.64" N, 91° 12'23.65" W.

Directions: About 4.5 miles northeast of Silver Bay on Hwy. 61. Located near mile marker 59.

Website: www.dnr.state.mn.us/state_parks/tettegouche

Waterway: Baptism River.

Height: 60 feet. **Crest:** Varies.

Nearest Town: Silver Bay.

Hike Difficulty: Moderate to strenuous.

Trail Quality: Good.

Round-trip Distance: 2–3 miles depending on your choice of trail.

Admission: A day pass at the state park is $5; a year-long pass (good at all state parks) is $25.

Trip Report & Tips: To find Two-Step Falls, drive over to the main campground and park in the parking lot. There you will have the choice of taking the Superior Hiking Trail or you can walk through the campground and take a shortcut to the falls. (See the park map for details.) . If you take the Superior Hiking Trail you'll come to a viewing platform for High Falls and a suspension bridge. There, on the east side of the bridge, you'll find a trail that says Two-Step Falls. The hike involves many steps; personally, I think Two-Step Falls should be called 200-step falls because the steps never seem to end. Eventually you'll see the falls, which are made up of two sections; the top step is much wider and taller than the second step. When the water level is low, you can easily see how the river gracefully cascades down over the reddish bedrock.

Bridge Cascades on the Manitou River

Location: George H. Crosby Manitou State Park.

Address/GPS for the Falls: 7616 Lake Cty. Rd. 7, Finland, 55603; 47° 28'50.63" N, 91° 5'52.88" W.

Directions: Off of Hwy. 61 by mile marker 59, turn north on Hwy. 1 and travel 6.1 miles to the little village of Finland. After you cross over the Baptism River, turn right on Cty. Rd. 7 and drive 7.5 miles. You will be on blacktop the first 1.2 miles and the rest is a well-maintained gravel road. Look for the state park sign; turn right and go a half mile back to a large parking lot.

Website: www.dnr.state.mn.us/state_parks/george_crosby_manitou

Waterway: Manitou River.

Height: Cascades vary from 2–5 feet. **Crest:** 25 feet.

Nearest Town: Finland.

Hike Difficulty: Moderate on the way to the cascades, but very strenuous back to the parking lot.

Trail Quality: Fair to poor.

Round-trip Distance: 3.4 miles, if you hike in on the Yellow Birch Trail.

Admission: A day pass at the state park is $5.

Trip Report & Tips: Start off from the parking lot, and be sure to pick up a park trail map. From there, you want to head to the backcountry campsite #5 via the Yellow Birch Trail. It connects to several others, so keep the map handy. From there, hike upstream for approximately 0.2 mile. Ahead you will see the rusty red Superior Hiking Trail bridge. Cross over the bridge and enjoy the thunderous roar of the falls. I call these the Bridge Cascades. If you go upstream, be sure to stop at the Manitou River Cascades (page 116) if you haven't done so.

Table Rock Falls, Manitou River

Location: George H. Crosby Manitou State Park.

Address/GPS for the Falls: 7616 Lake Cty. Rd. 7, Finland, 55603; 47° 28'40.13" N, 91° 5'44.05" W.

Directions: Off of Hwy. 61 by mile marker 59, turn north on Hwy. 1 and travel 6.1 miles to the little village of Finland. After you cross over the Baptism River, turn right on Cty. Rd. 7 and drive 7.5 miles. You will be on blacktop the first 1.2 miles and the rest is a well-maintained gravel road. Look for the state park sign; turn right and go a half mile back to a large parking lot.

Website: www.dnr.state.mn.us/state_parks/george_crosby_manitou

Waterway: Unnamed inlet stream.

Height: 12–15 feet. **Crest:** 2–3 feet.

Nearest Town: Finland.

Hike Difficulty: Moderate.

Trail Quality: The trails leading to the vicinity are fine, but there's no official trail to the falls themselves.

Round-trip Distance: 1.8 miles.

Admission: A day pass at the state park is $5.

Trip Report & Tips: From the parking lot, take the Yellow Birch Trail for an easy 0.9-mile hike. After a few minutes into your hike you'll cross a wooden bridge, which is followed by a boardwalk. At 0.9 mile, the trail becomes Misquah Trail. Take a left by the bench and head down 7 wooden steps where you will find a picturesque stream and a footbridge. To find the Table Rock waterfall, head back up the steps and take an immediate left at the top of the hill into the woods. Warning: There is no path. Follow your ears to the sound of the waterfall, which has a fairytale feel.

Two Island Falls, Two Island River

Location: Just north of Taconite Harbor.

Address/GPS for the Falls: 47° 31'32.78" N, 90° 55'37.50" W.

Directions: 2 miles south of Schroeder, just north of Taconite Harbor near mile marker 77. Park on the side of Hwy. 61 next to Two Island River.

Website: None.

Waterway: Two Island River.

Height: 25 feet. **Crest:** Varies.

Nearest Town: Schroeder.

Hike Difficulty: Easy. **Trail Quality:** Good.

Round-trip Distance: 0.4 mile to main falls; additional falls located below the Hwy. 61 bridge.

Admission: None.

Trip Report & Tips: Follow the worn path through birch trees, bushes, tall grass and young evergreens. Go up and down a couple small hills and cross over the railroad tracks. Here you'll find little iron ore pellets sprinkled in between the railroad ties. After crossing the tracks you'll see a good-sized waterfall. The water plummets about 25 feet down into a pool, and then goes under the railroad tracks through two huge culverts and cascades downhill across huge boulders. Down closer to the highway you'll see some cool trees growing out of rocks. There are also "potholes" in the ancient lava rock that are fun and interesting to check out. This is a great waterfall to view after the spring runoff when the water is really flowing. If you have time, walk downstream and check out the Hwy. 61 culvert on the left side down to the lower part of the river. Here you'll find some more small falls.

Triple Falls, Two Island River

Location: Just north of Taconite Harbor.

Address/GPS for the Falls: 47° 31'40.05" N, 90° 55'52.77" W.

Directions: Drive into a narrow gravel driveway just south of Two Island River. It's on the west side of Hwy 61. You can park your vehicle in the small parking area that's 0.1 mile down the road and hike the 0.3 mile up to the second set of railroad tracks. You can also drive up the narrow minimum-maintenance road for a total of 0.4 mile. I chose not to drive because I didn't want my Suburban to get scratched.

Website: None.

Waterway: Two Island River.

Height: 4 feet, 5 feet and 9 feet. **Crest:** Varies.

Nearest Town: Schroeder.

Hike Difficulty: Easy. **Trail Quality:** Good.

Round-trip Distance: 0.7 mile.

Admission: None.

Trip Report & Tips: It's an easy 0.3-mile walk up the minimum-maintenance road. The road meanders a bit but eventually meets a set of railroad tracks. Hike up the ditch, cross the tracks (though be mindful of passing trains), and you'll then see beautiful Upper Two Island Falls off to your left. If you hike up on either side of the falls, you'll be welcomed by three more falls that I call Triple Falls. I chose to rock-climb up along the right side of Upper Falls along with my daring friend Jessica. We got to the top and we were happy to have made the effort! Up near the falls, the river is about 20 feet wide. The first falls drop 4 feet, the middle falls come down 5 feet and then the river swings over to the left and pinches to 4 feet wide and drops down 9 more feet.

Upper Poplar River Falls

Upper Poplar River Cascades

Upper Falls and Cascades, Poplar River

Location: Superior Hiking Trail.

Address/GPS for the Falls: 445 Ski Hill Rd., Lutsen, 55612; 47° 40'0.73" N, 90° 43'19.30" W.

Directions: Off of Hwy. 61 just past the Lutsen Resort sign by mile marker 90, turn north on Lutsen Mt. Ski Hill Rd. Drive 2 miles to the end of the road. You'll be passing by all the Lutsen ski buildings. Park in the Superior Hiking Trail gravel parking lot.

Website: None.

Waterway: Poplar River.

Height: Varies. **Crest:** Varies.

Nearest Town: Lutsen.

Hike Difficulty: Easy. **Trail Quality:** Good.

Round-trip Distance: 0.25 miles.

Admission: None.

Trip Report & Tips: From the parking lot you'll want to take the gravel trail to the left and head down the gradual hill. After only a three-minute hike you'll come to the bridge overlooking the cascades upstream and the falls downstream. The sign by the bridge says "BRIDGE CLOSED, pedestrians only." The wide-mouthed river cascades over many boulders, flowing into a narrow 15-foot chute under the wooden pedestrian bridge and downward heading southeast. The boulders near the bridge are enormous and would be fun to climb on, but the river was a little crazy the May day that I was hiking. As the river heads downward, it forms some awesome rapids and then plummets to form more short falls as it drops among the poplars and dark volcanic rocks. The famous Superior National Golf Course and the historic Lutsen Resort are also just down the road.

Hidden Falls, Cascade River

Location: Cascade River State Park.

Address/GPS for the Falls: 47° 44'36.16" N, 90° 31'38.52" W.

Directions: About 6.5 miles from Cascade River State Park. To get there, head east on Hwy. 61 for 1.7 miles, turn left on Cty. Rd. 7 and go north 1.9 miles. Then turn left and head north on Cty. Rd. 44 for 0.5 mile. Take another left on Hwy. 45 (Pike Lake Rd.) and drive west 2.6 miles until you see the Hwy. 45 bridge over the Cascade River. The Superior Hiking Trail parking lot is off to the right.

Website: None.

Waterway: Cascade River.

Height: Flows down for a few hundred feet.

Crest: Varies.

Nearest Town: Grand Marais.

Hike Difficulty: Easy. **Trail Quality:** Fair.

Round-trip Distance: 0.6 mile.

Admission: None.

Trip Report & Tips: From the Superior Hiking Trail parking lot you'll need to head under the bridge and first admire the cool graffiti. Start hiking the Superior Hiking Trail across some boards, crazy roots and through the interesting old cedar trees; this is some of the prettiest terrain on the Cascade River. At 0.3 mile in you'll see the Hidden Falls on your right. It's hard to get a good image of the falls since they cascade down over a couple hundred feet and in a deep, narrow gorge. When we visited on May 19th, the water was wild. I looked downstream and saw a 120–150-foot skinny, ephemeral waterfall coming down from the top of the canyon walls. It was amazing and I knew it wouldn't be there for long. Also, be on the lookout for wildlife; while we were driving on Pike Lake Rd., a wolf jumped out of the ditch in front of us and crossed the road.

Cut Face Creek Falls

Location: Cut Face Creek Wayside Rest.

Address/GPS for the Falls: 47° 43'56.65" N, 90° 26'43.38" W.

Directions: Located near mile marker 104 on Hwy. 61 just 5 miles southwest of my favorite town, Grand Marais. Park at the wayside rest.

Website: None.

Waterway: Cut Face Creek.

Height: 8–12 feet. **Crest:** 8 feet.

Nearest Town: Grand Marais.

Hike Difficulty: Easy and fun, but put your boots on.

Trail Quality: Poor.

Round-trip Distance: 0.5 mile.

Admission: None.

Trip Report & Tips: From the wayside rest parking lot, cross over to the other side of Hwy. 61. From there, climb down to the creek, which is due west of the parking lot. It's very pretty once you get back into the tucked-away valley. After a couple of bends in the creek you'll come to the peaceful falls area. Here the falls are only 8 feet wide, but it is very picturesque. The flowing water is calming and refreshing. Hiking up the rocky creek bed is fun and adventurous at any time of year, though keep in mind that if you visit when the water levels are low (summer!), you might not find much water, or the falls. But when the water is flowing, they are a lovely sight.

Old Cedar Falls, Fall River

Location: Just outside Grand Marais.

Address/GPS for the Falls: 47° 44'32.55" N, 90° 23'18.05" W.

Directions: On Hwy. 61, 2 miles south of Grand Marais at mile marker 107.

Website: None.

Waterway: Fall River.

Height: 8 feet. **Crest:** Varies.

Nearest Town: Grand Marais.

Hike Difficulty: Moderate to difficult; especially steep if you are going down to river level.

Trail Quality: Poor.

Round-trip Distance: 0.2 mile.

Admission: None.

Trip Report & Tips: Park on the north side of Hwy. 61 by the guardrail. Follow the path along the guardrail, then turn right. If the water levels are high, there may be a small creek you need to hop over. From there, head up a short, but steep, hill to photograph or view Old Cedar Falls as it tumbles through the rocky gorge surrounded by tall pines and cedars. If you look closely, you'll see the upper set of falls that I call its Middle Falls. You can view these if the river is really flowing heavily. As the water cascades toward you, it flows over some very colorful stones. These falls are great to visit if the water level is up, and levels can change quickly, giving the same falls an entirely different look and feel in a matter of days. From your vantage point high up, you can head directly down to the river, depending on the water level and how wet you want to get. On one early evening visit, my girls and I were able to hike down with our rain boots on. It's a fun and secluded area to explore.

Colvill Falls

Location: Just outside Colvill.

Address/GPS for the Falls: 47° 47'34.19" N, 90° 9'53.70" W.

Directions: Off Hwy. 61 on the west end of Colvill. Just west of the Colvill sign on the north side of the road. Near mile marker 118.

Website: None.

Waterway: Unnamed creek; spring run-off.

Height: 12–15 feet. **Crest:** Varies.

Nearest Town: Colvill.

Hike Difficulty: Moderate; you can hike up the shallow falls with boots on or hike up on the grass next to the falls and then do a short, steep climb to the creek.

Trail Quality: There's no real trail here.

Round-trip Distance: 0.1 mile.

Admission: None.

Trip Report & Tips: A little gem tucked among red rocks along Hwy. 61., I believe this may just be an ephemeral waterfall, one that only pops up after the snow melts in the hills. After driving by the location many times, I never noticed it until the spring of 2015. Still, the waterfall is of significant size and cascades down over many layers of red chiseled rock. The jagged rocky face is set deep back in the red canyon walls. I have not heard or read about this waterfall anywhere else, so because of that, I've dubbed it Colvill Falls.

Tree-Hugger Falls, Kadunce River

Location: Park at the Kadunce River Wayside (also spelled Kodonce).

Address/GPS for the Falls: 47° 47'52.70" N, 90° 9'25.16" W.

Directions: Just 18 miles northeast of Grand Marais; located at mile marker 118.7.

Website: None.

Waterway: Kadunce River.

Height: 6 feet. **Crest:** Varies.

Nearest Town: Colvill.

Hike Difficulty: Moderate to strenuous if you head down the steep area to the falls; getting to the gorge itself is fairly easy hiking.

Trail Quality: Good to fair; some steps, roots and rocks to hike over.

Round-trip Distance: 0.4 mile.

Admission: None.

Trip Report & Tips: From the wayside parking lot, cross over Hwy. 61 and look for the Superior Hiking Trail sign. Start hiking up alongside the river. At 0.1 mile into your hike you'll go up 21 wooden steps. After you've walked 0.2 mile, you'll see a sign on your left that says "Don't throw rocks into the gorge." Head down the very steep hill immediately after the sign. You'll see why I call it Tree-Hugger Falls, as you'll need to grab a branch and scoot down on the rocks. It's really not quite as bad as it looks. As you get closer, the water plummets down a short 6 feet and then the river takes a 180-degree turn by a really tall jagged, rocky wall. After you've examined the area down in the gorge and you've checked out the huge rocky indentations, it's time to hoof it back up to the top.

Lower Falls, Brule River

Location: Judge C. R. Magney State Park.

Address/GPS for the Falls: 4051 E Hwy. 61, Grand Marais, 55604; 47° 49'30.13" N, 90° 2'58.69" W.

Directions: Near mile marker 124.

Website: None.

Waterway: Brule River.

Height: Cascades down 15–20 feet. **Crest:** Varies.

Nearest Town: Hovland.

Hike Difficulty: Moderate. **Trail Quality:** Good to fair.

Round-trip Distance: 1.5 miles.

Admission: A day pass at the state park is $5. A yearly vehicle pass is $25 and allows you to enter all state parks for a year.

Trip Report & Tips: From the Judge Magney parking lot, follow the trail to the Devil's Kettle. First you'll cross over the green bridge that goes over the Brule River, and at 0.3 mile into the hike you'll come to a set of 21 steps. After hiking 0.5 mile, there will be a spur trail to your left; take it and head down toward the river. Here you'll have a lovely view of the Upper Falls off in the distance. With the Upper Falls in front of you and the benches behind you, head down into the woods to your left. The trail branches off into three new paths, each leading to the Lower Falls. You can either walk along the steep ridge or pick a path over a little bit to the left. After 0.1 mile you'll come to a bench and then 22 wooden steps. The trail will become steep and narrow. You'll hear the river roaring on both sides; there is a really cool lookout at the end of the trail.

Flute Reed River Falls

Location: Near Hovland.

Address/GPS for the Falls: 47° 50'35.29" N, 89° 57'47.68" W.

Directions: Park along the side of Hwy. 61, just north of the Chicago Bay Marketplace Bakery. This is near the highway signs for the Arrowhead Trail and the Flute Reed River.

Website: None.

Waterway: Flute Reed River.

Height: Each of the 3 waterfalls is 3–5 feet high.

Crest: 6 feet, 12–15 feet and 4 feet, respectively.

Nearest Town: Hovland.

Hike Difficulty: Easy.

Trail Quality: Fair. Follow a trail down the ditch and hike across the rocks down by the riverside.

Round-trip Distance: 0.1 mile

Admission: None.

Trip Report & Tips: These aren't amazing waterfalls, but it is a wonderfully fun area to photograph and very easy to access. The Flute Reed River crosses under North Rd. three times, then goes under Hwy. 61 and out to Lake Superior, and its course features rapids, cascades and mini-waterfalls the whole way. So pick a spot, and start exploring in May after the spring rains and snow melt. To access the falls from the highway you'll want to choose a path and head down to the river, where you will find three small falls areas. Depending on the water level, you can walk alongside the river on the big flat brownish-gray stacked rocks. When the water levels are up, the river is worth witnessing (albeit from a distance). Once you're done with the falls, take a gander at the rapids too. To reach them, head northeast on Hwy. 61, turn left on the Arrowhead Trail (Cook Cty. Rd. 16) for 0.1 mile. Then turn left on North Rd. for 0.1 mile. Cross the bridge going over the Flute Reed River and park your vehicle on the side of the road. There are all sorts of great vantage points from this area.

11 Tips for Enhancing Your Waterfall Experience

1. Bring Extra Gear: Pack backup gear for everything, from your clothes, boots, shoes and socks to all of your equipment. On all of my waterfall adventures, I've lost two tripods, my friend Rachel's hiking boot fell apart and we got a 100-foot tape measure stuck in The Cascades on the Baptism River, never to be unstuck again! I also had an old Canon G9 camera go underwater (not on purpose), and it didn't survive. Backup clothing is especially important, as you'll need it more often than not. You never know what's going to happen with the Minnesota weather, especially up north. Oh, and pack a couple of umbrellas too.

2. Filters: Invest in good camera filters. A neutral-density filter is very important when photographing waterfalls, and I like to put on a warming filter occasionally if I feel the environment is too cool in tone. A graduated neutral-density filter is also very helpful when creating an image that has a bright sky and a shaded scene. There are many different types of graduated neutral-density filters. I like the one that is 4x6 and I can hand hold it in front of my lens. One other must-have filter is a polarizer. This will help reduce reflections on the water, make skies more dramatic and will also block about 1.5 stops worth of light from reaching your camera. You should also invest in a nice pouch to keep all your spendy filters organized and safe.

3. Tripod: I almost feel like my opinion on tripods isn't worthy, since I lost two in the crazy spring rivers up north. Use a good tripod, but you don't need the best. You're going to want your tripod to be lightweight since you'll be carrying it for many miles. A sturdy ball-head will be just fine to hold your camera steady during those long exposures.

4. Time: You do not want to be rushed while at a waterfall. If you know you want sunset images, try to go a little earlier so you can figure out your vantage points and get all your gear in order before the sun actually starts to set.

5. Organization: This is so important. When I hike a waterfall for the first time, I need to know many things: The exact location of the park or waterfall is a must and hopefully this book will be a great guide for you. I also want to know how far of a hike it is. So this is what I do: On my hikes, I have my tripod, camera backpack, pedometer and my "shootsac." In the backpack is my camera, remote shutter-release cord, filters and sometimes an extra lens. The less weight in my backpack, the better. In my shootsac I carry a bottle of water, my cell phone, a compass, a whistle, bug spray, a notebook and pen, an extra filter, if needed, and a lens cleaning cloth. Around my neck I always carry my little Canon camera. At this time it's the Canon G16. I use this for video, trail and sign shots, scene setters and fun, silly pictures.

6. Footwear: Invest in good hiking boots, tennis shoes, Keens or sandals, and buy some rain boots with good traction. You'll be on lots of very rugged terrain and you'll be hiking over lots of roots and rocks. In the winter you may want to invest in some good snow shoes, cross country skis and some ice cleats for your boots.

7. Water: Always carry a bottle of water along with you, even if you think it's going to be a short hike. Sometimes it ends up being a long one!

8. Exploration: Explore early, explore often, explore late and explore all four seasons. Get up before the sun, and head out early for that beautiful morning light. It may be tough getting out of bed so early, but you'll always be glad you did. Explore these amazing waterfalls often. You can go visit a waterfall within weeks of your last visit and it can look substantially different, depending on rainfall and water levels. Explore late at night or at sunset. Try photographing a waterfall during the full moon and use the light of the moon for your images. Explore during all of Minnesota's beautiful four seasons. Each month will be different and some will be more dramatic than others. Last but not least, try to explore on overcast days for waterfall photography, as your images will look better.

9. Booking: Part of the fun of the waterfall experience is traveling around our great state and staying at different places. If you plan on a fall adventure, make sure to book your lodging at least a couple of months in advance. The North Shore resorts and cabins fill up quickly. One tip I can give you is to never drive up north on a Friday (the traffic is nuts) and don't come home on a Sunday. For example, Hwy. 61 only has two lanes, and the traffic is crazy during the peak fall season. My best advice is to go during the week, if you can, as there will be fewer people to get in your way.

10. Self-Assignments: My whole "explore Minnesota" venture began in April 2012 with a self-assignment to "photograph Minnesota" with my kids. Since I'm a portrait photographer with a studio in central Minnesota, this was a very big assignment. But it was great, and it turned into something wonderful: this book.

11. Safety: This one is by far the most important: Always use caution and keep safety in mind. Even though most of us love to climb rocks and explore every nook and cranny around, sometimes that's not the best thing to do. My best advice is to always use common sense. The first time my tripod fell off the slippery rocks, I was high above the Lester River. I could see the tripod leg poking out of the river in between the crashing waves against the rock. I could have gotten down and possibly grabbed it, but it wasn't worth my life or my daughter's. She was 10 years old at the time and really wanted to go down and get it. While it was a $300 tripod, I wasn't taking the chance of tumbling down into the frigid, rocky river. That's why I recommend that you always go hiking with a friend, carry a cellphone (and a whistle) and know how to deal with any contingency, whether it's a sudden rainstorm or a run-in with a bear.

On that note, I'll leave you with one more rule—have fun, and enjoy all of the amazing waterfalls Minnesota has to offer.

24 More Waterfalls to Explore

	GPS Coordinates	Location	Height
	Cannon Falls 44° 30'31.45"N 92° 54'26.79"W	In Cannon Falls at Minnieska Park on the Little Cannon River. Located on the west side of MN-20/4th St. N.	We measured the top falls at 5 feet. The whole falls cascade down about 12-15 feet.
	Minnemishinona Falls, Mankato 44° 10'12.22"N 94° 5'6.87"W	40923 Judson Bottom Road in Mankato.	42 feet.
	Hidden Falls, St. Paul 44° 54'35.28"N 93° 11'31.84"W	At Hidden Falls Regional Park, just across the Mississippi River from Minneha-ha Falls.	22 feet.
	Shadow Falls, St. Paul 44° 56'32.16"N 93° 11'52.53"W	Shadow Falls Park Preserve is located at the intersection of Mississippi River Blvd. and the very western end of Summit Ave.	29 feet.
	Curtain Falls, Interstate State Park 45° 23'45.78"N 92° 40'23.01"W	Near the south entrance to Interstate State Park and mile marker 21 on Hwy. 95, just south of Taylors Falls.	38 feet.
	Hamm Memorial Waterfall, St. Paul 44° 58'56.61"N 93° 8'38.86"W	Como Park.	30 feet.

	GPS Coordinates	Location	Height
	Como Zoo Falls, St. Paul 44° 58'54.85"N 93° 9'9.75"W	In Como Park at the zoo.	5-6 feet.
	Normandale Lake Waterfall, Bloomington 44° 50'53.55"N 93° 21'5.54"W	On Normandale Blvd., just south of 84th St.	7 feet.
	Junction Bay Falls, Voyageurs National Park 48° 25'3.90"N 92° 40'10.39"W	You many need a guide to take you to this hidden gem in Junction Bay off of Namakan Lake.	30 feet.
	Earl Falls, Gunflint Trail 48° 6'50.19"N 90° 50'2.55"W	On Larch Creek just south of Sea Gull Guard Station and near the end of the Gunflint Trail.	4 feet.
	Keene Creek Falls, Duluth 46°45'7.19"N 92°11'12.03"W	Cross Highland St. bridge and turn right on Skyline Blvd and proceed for 0.3 mile. The falls will be on your right.	5 feet.
	Highland Bridge Falls, Keene Creek, Duluth 46° 44'53.69"N 92° 11'6.78"W	Park at the Skyline Blvd. parking lot near the Highland St. Bridge. Hike under the bridge and follow Keene Creek a short distance until you see the falls.	6-8 feet.

	GPS Coordinates	Location	Height
	Nude Swimming Hole Falls, Duluth 46° 51'14.69"N 92° 0'21.81"W	On the Lester River 1.2 miles up Lester Road from Superior St. Bridge in Duluth.	10 feet.
	Two Sisters Waterfall, Duluth 46° 51'25.69"N 91° 59'59.70"W	On the Lester River 1.3 miles up Lester Road from Superior St. Bridge in Duluth.	8-12 feet.
	Barrier Falls, Devil Track River 47° 46'44.31"N 90° 17'7.51"W	1.4 miles up the Devil Track River or follow the Superior Hiking Trail to the Barrier Falls lookout.	30 feet.
	First Falls, Knife River 46° 56'48.16"N 91° 47'36.50"W	South of mile marker 18 on the Hwy. 61 Expressway.	Varies.
	Shovel Point Falls at Tettegouche State Park 47° 20'21.48"N 91° 11'27.67"W	Tettegouche State Park.	25 feet.
	Last Creek Falls 44° 30'31.45"N 92° 54'26.79"W	From Taconite Harbor, view from the boat on your way down to see the mouth of the Manitou River waterfall.	Varying heights cascade down.

	GPS Coordinates	Location	Height
	More Caribou Falls, Caribou River 47° 28'16.27"N 91° 1'59.44"W	Just upstream from the Superior Hiking Trail bridge located 0.7 mile from Caribou River Wayside.	Varies.
	Bike Bridge Falls, Lutsen 47° 38'20.09"N 90° 42'29.22"W	On the Poplar River by mile marker 90 on Hwy. 61 right across from the Lutsen Resort sign.	Varies.
	Lower Falls, Devil Track River 47° 46'42.78"N 90° 16'41.77"W	1.1 miles up the Devil Track River.	7-9 feet.
	Elizabeth Dam, Elizabeth 46° 22'47.69"N 96° 7'33.05"	On the east edge of town by the Co. Rd. 10 bridge.	15 feet.
	Terrace Mill, Terrace 45° 30'40.96"N 95° 19'15.82"W	27165 Old Mill Pond Road, Terrace.	Slopes down under bridge approx. 12-15 feet.
	Phelps Mill, Underwood 46° 22'49.22"N 95° 49'16.80"W	29035 Co. Hwy. 45, Underwood.	8 feet and 103 feet long.

About the Author

I was born and raised in Hutchinson and got my first camera at the age of 11. My models included Mittsie, my blue-eyed black lab, all my stuffed animals and dolls, my dad with his tractors and pigs, and my brother with his GMC S15 truck and his sheep. In 11th grade, Media Tech was an elective class that helped me learn more about filmcameras. After high school I chose the professional photography program at Willmar Technical College and studied portrait and commercial photography for two years. After graduation I worked for Sue Dropp for five years at Dropp's Unique Photography in Waite Park. I learned a lot about the portrait world of photography and decided to open up my own studio in April 1999. Country Gallery is located on 10 beautifully landscaped acres in central Minnesota. We photograph families, children, pets, high school seniors, school sports teams, and charity events. In April 2012 I gave myself the assignment to "photograph Minnesota." It's been a fun traveling adventure that has led me down many different roads, both literally and figuratively.

All in all, I do what I love and thoroughly enjoy my profession. It gives me great flexibility with my schedule and offers me a wide variety of subjects and places to photograph.

Notes

Notes

Notes

Notes